THIS IS
THE FIRE

ALSO BY DON LEMON

Transparent

THIS IS THE FIRE

What I Say to My Friends About Racism

DON LEMON

Little, Brown and Company

New York   Boston   London

Little, Brown and Company
Hachette Book Group
1290 Avenue of the Americas, New York, NY 10104
littlebrown.com

First Edition: March 2021

Little, Brown and Company is a division of Hachette Book Group, Inc. The Little, Brown name and logo are trademarks of Hachette Book Group, Inc.

The publisher is not responsible for websites (or their content) that are not owned by the publisher.

The Hachette Speakers Bureau provides a wide range of authors for speaking events. To find out more, go to hachettespeakersbureau .com or call (866) 376-6591.

ISBN 978-0-316-25757-2 (hardcover) / 978-0-316-27352-7 (large print) / 978-0-316-26544-7 (Barnes & Noble signed) / 978-0-316-26554-6 (signed)

LCCN 2020949934

Printing 1, 2021

LSC-C

Printed in the United States of America

*To the memory of those who paved the way,
with gratitude to those who march in their footsteps:
James Baldwin, my sister Leisa, and all the
not-so-obvious heroes
who daily take a stand for truth.*

Contents

THIS IS
THE FIRE

Prologue

A Letter to My Nephew

May 25, 2020

Dear Trushaad,

Today I heard a dying man call out to his mama, and I wept for the world that will soon belong to you. I know what comes next as surely as I know the Mississippi rolls down to the sea.

The weeping passes, and rage takes hold.

The rage burns out, and blame begins.

The blame bounces back and forth, and promises are made.

The promises wither, and complacency returns.

And the complacency stays. It stagnates like a lullaby on autoplay, until another man dies facedown on another street in another city, and the weeping begins again.

I was the baby boy in our family until thirteen years ago, when you came along and made a grandmother of my big sister Leisa. Your grandmother helped raise me, and I helped raise your mother, so when you were born, it all came full circle. You look like me. We share the same forehead, nose, and well-articulated arm bones. We share the same skin, a dark russet color rich with history. Yours is darker than mine in winter, but in the summertime, I gravitate in your direction.

"I know you," I said the first time I saw you.

You made me believe I was beautiful, because there was not one thing I would change about you—not the kinky hair I had tried so hard to relax, nor the tapered nose that failed to match my father's, and no, absolutely not that rich russet skin. My hope, then and now, is for you to embrace your beautiful Blackness with an ease I never mastered, no matter how many times your grandmother told me I was a thing of beauty.

I spent my early childhood in the home of my own grandmother, Mame (pronounced *mah-ME*), who was a wonder. She could balance the world in a laundry basket, bake cathead biscuits, and tell a great story, all at the same time.

"Before Dr. King and the Freedom Riders and all that, we go to vote, and the poll watcher, he says, 'Naw, you gotta first pay this money,' so you pay that money, and then he says, 'Okay, you gotta tell me—how many jelly beans in this here jar. How many soap bubbles in a bar of soap.' Meanwhile, you see White people walk up. 'Oh, hello! Yes, ma'am. Sign here. Go right on in.' Things went on that I can't even tell you."

If you couldn't prove you had more than a fifth-grade education, which is all Mame had, the state of Louisiana required a literacy test. Between bold lines across the top, it said:

Do what you are told to do in each statement, nothing more, nothing less. Be careful as one wrong answer denotes failure of the test. You have 10 minutes to complete the test.

A convoluted list of questions followed.

Draw a line around the number or letter of this sentence.

In the first circle below, write the last letter of the first word that starts with L.

In the space below, draw three circles, one engulfed by another.

I couldn't comprehend such a thing. I kept asking her about it, trying to make sense of it, and one day I broke down crying, overwhelmed by the realness of life for people like us. There was something deeply, terribly wrong—something much bigger than a house or a sugarcane factory or Louisiana itself. I didn't know how to change it, but I knew Mame struggled with her reading, so I eagerly learned to read, wanting to help her. We played school at her kitchen table.

That was education for my grandmother. My mother went to a segregated school. My big sisters went to integrated public schools. I went to an all-Black Catholic school, and now you go to a mostly White laboratory school, where they test-drive advances in education theory and technology. I wonder what Mame would say if she could see the computers and green spaces.

I want to celebrate that arc, but the fact of how far we've come only serves to highlight how far back we started and how far we've yet to go.

One circle engulfed by another.

The day you were born, I saw Leisa take up the mantle of a Black grandmother, and I understood something I was too little to know about Mame. I saw the protective stance of my sister—the power of her tenderness, the ferocity of her love—and I felt the embrace of all these formidable women who hold our family in their arms. From the moment of my birth, they sheltered me. From the moment of your birth, I was wise enough to know the preciousness of that stronghold and the price they paid for it.

Tru, the man who died—his name was George—he begged for that embrace when he could no longer beg for breath. He called for his mama as he felt the last of his life unravel. The last thread left between his body and soul was love, and as terrible as this was to witness, it spurred a tidal swell of love in me. For my mama. For Mame. For my sisters. For you, TruTru, and for your little cousin Cairo.

Weeping.

Rage.

Blame.

Promises.

Complacency.

If our last honest breath is not love, I don't know how we live to fight through it all again.

I need to believe we'll wake up, rise up, and stay standing this time. My greatest fear is that the

world will jade itself and grow numb, that the
death rattle of a man who looks like you and me
will no longer move the world to tears, that there
will be no tears left, no purifying rage, no chafing
blame, no hopeful promise—only the wax-
museum visage of complacency.

You're old enough to know what's going on,
approaching the precipice where you'll begin to
understand. Soon you'll see the difference between
those who preach, those who march, and those
who maintain a deferential silence while the
bullhorn of racism blares the same foul tropes it's
been sounding for four hundred years. I promise
you, Tru, because I love you: I will not stand
among the silent. Silence is no longer an option.

1

Do I But Dream

A comfortable two-hour drive from the Midtown head-quarters of CNN, not far from the Sag Harbor home I share with my fiancé, Tim, a truncated boardwalk path cuts through the dune grass and gives way to tawny sand on the beach at Sag Harbor Bay. A stone marker at the trailhead honors the founder of this extraordinary enclave, an African American neighborhood on prime beachfront real estate.

"In grateful recognition of Maude K. Terry," it says. "Do I but dream."

Docile green waves lap at the shore where Indigenous people, the Shinnecock, withstood bleak pre-Columbian winters and bloody raids by the neighboring Pequot until Europeans arrived on the continent in the 1500s, bringing

Bibles and smallpox. The Shinnecock had no immunity to the virus, of course, and little energy left over to resist the Holy Spirit. Two-thirds of their population was wiped out within a few years. Able-bodied survivors went to work on Melvillesque whaling vessels, some of which were outfitted for the clandestine purpose of "blackbirding": the acquisition, by coercion or outright kidnapping, of Indigenous people from faraway islands and coastal regions to labor on cotton and sugar plantations in Europe and the Colonies.

In July 1619, legislative representatives from eleven large New World settlements met in Jamestown, Virginia, to establish the standards and practices that would lay a foundation for the democracy they aspired to build. One month later, at nearby Point Comfort, about two dozen Angolan men and women were offloaded and sold by Portuguese slave traders. Thus the dream of democracy and the nightmare of slavery were born in the same urgent breath, and there was never a time when White people, as a monolith, were comfortable with it. There were always agitators and conscientious objectors; they just couldn't summon the traction needed to overcome the landed gentry and wealthy industrialists who depended on free labor for their beefy bottom line.

Fast-forward a century and a half. An early draft of the Declaration of Independence condemned slavery as "piratical warfare" and an "assemblage of horrors"—a "cruel war against human nature itself"—but 33-year-old Thomas Jefferson and his young allies were shouted down by older, more pragmatic voices who agreed in theory with all that "inalienable rights" jazz but argued that their cotton wasn't going to pick itself. If there was any discussion of extending these rights to women of any color, it has vanished from history. The document was revised to a "sorry, not sorry" declaration of the independence of White men.

> We hold these truths to be self-evident, that all men
> are created equal...

They said this without a wink. Utterly sincere. Perhaps the only way to reconcile their lofty ideals and barbaric actions was to compartmentalize; slaves and savages could not be considered "men" in the strictest image-of-God sense. If the framers had seen these wretches as *men*, they would have been forced to see themselves as barbarians.

But when young Jefferson went on to write the Preamble to the Constitution, he left a ticking time bomb: a single adverb that should unsettle every generation and inspire every striver, and on this they all agreed. Our brilliant founders set, for themselves and posterity, the task of forming "a more perfect union." Not perfect. *More* perfect. The quest for perfect is a doomed endeavor—a plastic cover on the sofa, artificial gardenias in a graveyard. Down that path lies despair, fatigue, familiar refrains about "just the way it is," and a thousand other excuses to give up.

The quest for *more* perfect is work ever in progress with no side door for laziness or apathy. *More perfect* is a call to action, a mandate for change, and this is where Miss Maude Terry comes in.

Fast-forward again, over nearly two centuries, through several generations of "manifest destiny," a few zealous revolutions, one population-culling flu pandemic, and a War to End All Wars, followed by a Second War to End All Wars, because—let's face it—making war does not end wars. Now we've arrived in pre–*Mad Men* America, land of Bettie Page sausage bangs, Bakelite jewelry, and atomic lampshades. The wartime economy was a rising tide. Black men who served in the military were going to college on the GI Bill, and Black women who worked alongside Rosie the Riveter were more financially solvent than they'd ever been. These people were strivers. A Black middle class burgeoned into being.

In 1947, Miss Maude Terry, a Black schoolteacher who was born in Lynchburg, Virginia, and made her way north to Brooklyn, found herself approaching the age of retirement and saw no reason why Black people should not spend their golden years on the beach if they so desired. She scouted out a twenty-acre swath of land on Long Island's marshy waterfront, a stretch considered "undesirable" in the midcentury real estate market. She reached out to the property owner's wife with an ambitious plan to subdivide the land. She found well-heeled Black buyers for the lots, which sold for $750 to $1,000. (Excuse me while I provide oxygen for Tim, a realtor who sees the same acreage priced in the millions today.)

"Redlining" and other racist financial practices buoyed segregation by preventing Black people from getting mortgages. So Maude Terry formed the Azurest Syndicate with her sister, Amaza Lee Meredith, one of the first African American women architects. Thus was born Azurest, one of the nation's oldest Black summer communities. Maude and Amaza jumped the turnstile of discrimination, brokered loans, and created the neighborhood close to the Sag Harbor home where Tim and I now plan to raise our family. We think Amaza and her life-partner, Edna, would be pleased. Back then, who would have dared to dream of a world in which "their kind" could marry? Tim and I would have been a double hard "no" back then, because he is White and I am Black. Interracial marriage— *exogamy! miscegenation!*—was explicitly criminalized in Apartheid South Africa, Nazi Germany, and the United States.

Until it wasn't.

* * * *

Change happens. A wilderness can be citified or a city xeriscaped, and as surely as outlaws become in-laws, the fundamental structure of a society can be reshaped. New ideas take root. Culture evolves.

We are experiencing a moment as terrifying and thrilling as any of the tectonic shifts that have borne us forward through history. I have to confess, even I didn't see it coming. A swift kick of reactionary zeal caught me by surprise, so I was not surprised at all when I saw a lot of White people react with startled knee-jerk aversity.

People keep saying, "This time feels different," and it does. It feels momentous—nothing less than the death throes of White supremacy in concert with the birth pangs of racial renaissance. Emotion is sweeping us forward, and I'm tremendously hopeful about our ability to harness this transformative energy. But public passion is a tide that ebbs and flows like the waves on Sag Harbor Bay, ever-changing, ever-changeless. Right now, social media has its hackles up, but that's a shallow hackle, lasting only a little longer than the flash-bang weapons hurled at the protesters. Those who seek to divide us, for fun and profit, are good at goosing outrage and then watering down the collective urge to actually do something.

Yes, this time feels different, but it won't *be* different unless we *make* it different with commitment, forbearance, and hard work. It's incumbent upon each of us to do something—*Do. Some. Damn. Thing.*—however brashly ambitious or seemingly inconsequential. It can't be performative. No selfie-mode ice-bucket-planking. We have to mean it. We have to live it. We've already had the discussion about front of the bus or back of the bus; now's the time to get on the bus or get left behind.

Looking back on the summer of 2020—or any other moment that feels like a moment of truth—and being forced to see ourselves through the unsparing lens of hindsight, every one of us will face a personal moment of reckoning:

I had an opportunity to know, and this is what I chose to believe.

I had an opportunity to speak, and this is what I chose to say.

I had an opportunity to act, and this is what I chose to do.

The shops and restaurants in our little community on Long Island, shuttered through the early months of the coronavirus pandemic, had begun to reopen like tentative amber snails, extending one tentacle at a time to feel out the humidity after an early summer storm. People were out walking with baby carriages and dogs. This end of Long Island is on the conservative side, so not everyone wore masks. Some people were clinging to the idea that following recommended guidelines was an unspoken indictment of the president who eschewed them. As if we didn't have enough dividing us, now we all had to pick sides in the masquerade: barefaced Trumpers on one side, Dr. Fauci followers on the other, trying to maintain a six-foot minimum distance.

The gravel crunched beneath my feet on my way to the boardwalk path. The beach was overcast and full of ghosts. Shinnecock whalers, perhaps, thinking, *Masks! Crap. Why didn't we think of that?* This is the sort of acerbic quip that crosses my mind when I get home from work at four in the morning.

The pandemic set the stage for everything that followed. In early spring 2020, the death toll ticked upward—one, fifteen, one thousand, one hundred thousand. With people of color disproportionately impacted, the public health crisis exposed gaping holes in services, food security, education, internet access, and a host of small things essential to human dignity. It lit up the chasm of opportunity between the haves and have-nots, revealing the fault lines and the foundations in our private domestic bubbles. It drew back the curtain on the creeping unkindness and tightfisted cronyism of an anti-intellectual administration.

On May 25, several panicked bystanders observed a 46-year-old Black man being held facedown on the pavement by four Minneapolis police officers. Through videos subsequently posted on Facebook, millions more bore witness. For more than five agonized minutes, one of the officers—posturing, cool and resolute—presses his knee on George Floyd's neck as Floyd groans, sobs, begs for breath, and calls out to his dead mother before he succumbs to an appalling stillness. The bystanders plead on Floyd's behalf, but the officer keeps his knee on Floyd's neck for another three minutes.

Watching this shocking footage, I and every other Black man I know saw the insensibly sluggish murder of ourselves. In agonized real time, I saw Billie Holiday's *strange fruit hanging from the poplar tree*. I had to close my door and cry.

But there was work to be done. The disturbing video went viral within hours, galvanizing multitudes who were emotionally raw from weeks of isolation and readily available to march, because the pandemic had shut down schools and workplaces. Protests that were overwhelmingly peaceful during the long summer days turned violent at night. This certainly was not the first time we heard the urgent plea—*"Black lives matter! Black lives matter! Black lives matter!"*—but the optics of George Floyd's death were so lurid and the circumstances so irrefutably egregious, it unleashed a riptide of grief and rage, exhumed the restless bones of massacred innocents in Tulsa and Rosewood, immolated the myth of desegregation, and dragged the untaught history of the United States out of the root cellar. It brought home an inkling—at last, at *least,* a glimpse—of Black suffering that White people were powerless to disclaim.

A moment like this comes only a few times in the career of any journalist. A story cracks open the sky and sunders whatever clouds hunker over us, a reverberating thunder followed by blinding flashes of light and electricity. History calls its witnesses. In these singular moments, the work of journalism is a calm, factual face that conceals the frantic endeavor of reportage. There's much to say about the courage and tenacity of the talented stringers and camera operators who took to the vans, masked superheroes risking their own health and safety without hesitation, as protesters poured into the streets of every major city in the United States.

The protests evoked comparisons to the 1960s, which gives some people hope while causing others to shrink from the stench of nostalgia. On one hand was the exhausted query, "Why are we still marching to resolve this shit?" On the other was validation and living proof that my sisters and their ilk have raised a generation of people who are fiercer, nobler, and more sincerely inclusive and boldly egalitarian than their elders. Thousands of young Americans lay on the pavement in full view of the White House, chanting the last words of George Floyd:

"I can't breathe. I can't breathe. I can't breathe."

The leadership vacuum laid bare by the pandemic was now at critical mass.

The first Saturday after George Floyd's death, Donald Trump gave a speech about a rocket launch. On Monday, he went briefly to his bunker under the White House and emerged late in the afternoon for a photo op in front of St. John's Episcopal Church on Lafayette Square, where protesters were cleared away with chemical repellent and nonlethal riot measures so he could march over there and pose holding up an apparently unused copy of the Bible — an eerie echo of the Europeans who arrived with their Bibles and a side order of syphilis.

In June, still disdaining the idea of wearing a face mask, he held a campaign rally in Tulsa, Oklahoma, where his campaign workers removed stickers that designated proper physical distancing. Turnout was dismal, so maybe it's coincidence that the rally was followed by a spike in the number of COVID-19 cases. In July he sent federal troops into American cities. More viral videos showed unidentified officers rousting unarmed protesters into unmarked vans.

Through the dog days of summer, Barack Obama talked about united efforts in the interest of public health, praised the overwhelmingly peaceful protesters, and advocated for meaningful police reform. Meanwhile, Trump complained that people wore masks because they didn't like him, denounced "thugs and looters," and repeatedly raised the specter of military "domination" of US citizens.

In August, we blew by one grim milestone after another: four million cases in the United States, 120,000 dead, 130,000 dead, 140,000 dead.

At the time, we thought that was a lot. That paradigm was about to shift.

James Baldwin's *The Fire Next Time* was published in 1963, as JFK was preparing to meet his destiny in Dallas, and Martin Luther King Jr. was praying for sleep on a fetid bunk in Birmingham City Jail. I wasn't born when Baldwin's book was written, and Baldwin was dead by the time I read it, so it was shocking how well he knew me. My first shopworn copy from the 1980s is still on my bookshelf. The margins are scrawled with mind-blown notes. Vehement underlining scores almost every page. The book itself is slender and elegant: 144 pages of vibrant storytelling, erudite commentary, dry wit, and uncanny vision. It begins with a sweetly gut-wrenching letter to his nephew and ends with a caveat that rings in my ears today, chilling and prescient: "If we do not now dare everything, the fulfillment of that prophecy, recreated from the Bible in song by a slave, is upon us: *God gave Noah the rainbow sign, No more water, the fire next time.*"

This is the fire. We're in it. JFK and Obama led us to the rainbow; Trump forced us into the fire. And then he poured gasoline on it.

If only he had responded sooner and more intelligently to the pandemic. If only he'd been an unaffected opportunist instead of a slumlord on steroids. If only he'd never taken out full-page newspaper ads calling for the deaths of innocent Black men. If only he had or had not made a thousand choices that resulted in a critical dearth of leadership at a moment when leadership was desperately needed.

If he'd set an example of competent, compassionate self-governance, we might have been able to ignore the mendacity of the toadies who govern under him. If our young people had not been forced to take to the streets, they might have been able to deny their destiny. Now, they can and must be the groundbreakers who fill this leadership vacuum before the world they are poised to inherit is reduced to a decaying city surrounded by plastic water bottles and unraked wilderness.

People kept saying, "This is a terrible moment to have a terrible president." I'll be the contrarian here. It breaks my heart and burns my tongue to say it, but in 2016, Donald Trump was exactly the president we deserved and probably the president we needed in the way you need symptoms that alert you to a disease. Racism is a cancer that has been metastasizing throughout this land ever since Columbus showed up. It's persisted because the right people had the luxury of ignoring it. Not anymore. With the election of a blatant White supremacist, the problem became palpable, impossible to ignore. It touches every one of us, because it's a detriment to every aspect of our society.

Trump was not our national lymphoma, he was the perseverating, malignant node in our armpit that finally forced us to acknowledge our worst fears and trudge our reluctant butts into the oncologist's office. We're in the waiting room now, our hearts pounding. We know this is bad, and it's going to get worse before it gets better, but we know that denial and foot-dragging—any attempt to avoid or delay the inevitably scorching cure—will lead to our demise.

Yes, you know. Come on, now. You do know.

You know how I know you know? Because of the Coopers.

On a crisp spring morning in May 2020, just two days after the death of George Floyd, Amy Cooper, a White investment banker, was walking her dog in a picturesque swath of New York City's Central Park called the Ramble. A West Coast acquaintance of mine keeps calling it the Bramble.

"No, it's the *Ramble*," I tell her, and then it occurs to me what a damn bramble it turned into that day.

Christian Cooper (no relation to Amy), an avid birdwatcher who happens to be Black, was also in the Ramble that morning, and he requested that Amy put her dog on a leash, as per park rules. He says he asked her politely; she says he yelled at her. It got contentious, and Chris took out his cell phone and started filming.

"I'm calling the cops," she warns. "I'm going to tell them there's an African American man threatening my life." Breathless, she paces, thumbing 911 into her phone, dragging the thrashing dog by its collar. "I'm in the Ramble, and there's a man—African American—he is recording me and threatening me and my dog." The dog flails in her grasp, mouthing her hand as she goes full La Scala, her voice trembling and breaking, an aria of faux tearstained anguish. "There is an *African American man*. I am in Central Park. Please send the cops immediately!"

After the video blew up on social media, Amy lost her job. And her dog. She released a statement: "I think I was just scared...I just want to publicly apologize to everyone...I'm not a racist. I did not mean to harm that man in any way...I don't mean to harm the African American community."

But this wasn't about the African American community. The way you treat other people is not about who *they* are; it's about who *you* are.

I wonder if she can hear her own statement in this context: First, there's the decision to walk the not-so-well-trained dog off its leash, because privilege, then the unwarranted zero-to-*Baby Jane* escalation. And then she references, in so many words, the mutual understanding that a Black man has good reason to fear the cops and she does not.

I asked Chris, "Do you accept her apology?"

"I think her apology is sincere," he said. "I'm not sure she recognizes that, while she may not be—or consider herself—as a racist, that particular act was definitely racist. The fact that *that* was her recourse at the moment—granted, it was a stressful situation, a sudden situation, maybe a moment of spectacularly poor judgment—but she went there."

I pointed out that her judgment was not so impaired as to keep her from connecting the dots between "cops" and "scary Black dude."

"She understood the power she wielded at that moment," I observed.

"Exactly," said Chris. "She was looking for some way to get an edge in the situation, and that's where she went. And that ultimately did not help her. So is she a racist? I can't answer that. Only she can answer that, and I would submit, probably the only way she's going to answer that is going forward, you know—how she conducts herself and how she chooses to reflect on this situation and examine it."

I would have been happy to sit down with Amy Cooper—or perhaps go for a walk with her in the Ramble. We invited her on the show, but she declined. I suspect her life had become a blizzard of internet shaming and ulcerating regret. There are people who can be reached and people who cannot be reached, and I would like to think most people probably can be. Confronted with such a "come to Jesus" moment, I'd like to assume that any reasonable person would want to do better and is at least willing to try. Whenever I hear someone say, "But I'm not racist!" I want to hear their desire to separate themselves from racism.

I know, that denial always evokes Queen Gertrude's dry assessment of an overzealous bit player in *Hamlet*: "The lady doth protest too much." But here's the thing: I don't care.

White brothers and sisters: Pocket that *But I'm Not Racist!* card. I don't want to hear about your Black girlfriend in college, or your Black postman to whom you give fruitcake every Christmas, or that Black comp and lit teacher who totally, like, rocked your world. It doesn't matter if you are racist or not racist or anti-racist; *our society is racist*. You're just letting me know how okay you are with that. If you're still in denial about it, then clearly you're comfortable with the way things are, and when you tell me you're not a racist, you're really telling me, "Please, stop talking about racism. Your oppression is harshing my mellow."

Acknowledging that we have a problem is the first step to solving it. So let's start by laying down the ludicrous construct that America has in any way dealt with the dire properties of endemic, systemic racism; the economically and psychologically ravaging legacy of slavery; or the slick-fingered perfidy of Jim Crow. This did not begin with George Floyd's face on the pavement, and it will not end with his face on a Jumbotron. He was the flash point, not the conflagration.

When I say we live in a system of White supremacy, I'm not just talking about cartoon White supremacy—hooded villains marching with ropes and torches—I'm talking about an entrenched socioeconomic system that statistically favors White consumers, White businesses, White stories, White iconography, White male politicians and power brokers, and a widely accepted version of vigorously scrubbed White history. I'm talking about the innocuous mashed-potato racism we swallow every day without chewing. It goes down easy until you notice it's full of broken glass.

Our pandemic zeitgeist left us simultaneously masked and unmasked. There's no "getting back to normal." No more "just lie there and think of England" like a cold-warring couple who claim they're staying together for the sake of the children when, in truth, they're just too cheap, lazy, and change-averse to do the work of accepting responsibility and resolving their anger so everyone can move on to a better life.

The Republicans knew Trump was an ill-behaved, bigoted pussy hound, but they supported him because #winning and then seemed dismayed that it was difficult to keep him on a leash. When we asked them nicely to abide by the rules, they responded with imperious displeasure. *Who are you to tell us what to do? Don't you know who we think we are?* When firmly reminded that they themselves made the rules for our so-called civilized world—*do unto others* and *we the people* and all that—they responded with aggrieved lip service. They yanked their mutt's chain and reprimanded him in hushed tones, forgetting that he speaks the language of conciliation about as well as a spaniel speaks banker. Finally, faced with the unblinking gaze of a hundred thousand cameras, backed into a corner by their own vitriol, they responded with rage. They defaulted to racism. They called the cops. They courted violence.

And so, here we are. Again.

Any time the streets are rife with willful resistance, it's heartening to hear people questioning the old, opening themselves to the new, and talking about *purpose*—that specific thing each of us is uniquely qualified and incontrovertibly called to do—asking in earnest, "What am *I* supposed to do about it?"

For me, the answer is this book, and in it, I hope you will find a springboard for your own call to purpose. In these pages, I'll share a few of the stories that have moved me most profoundly, cut me most deeply, and caused me to examine the contents of my own heart. These American parables are all slivers of human experience that, when taken together, speak to the toxicity of racism and call us out with specific personal and societal mandates. As a journalist, I am tasked with the telling of it all. Day after day, I do what I was trained to do: gather information, weed out the BS, set bias aside, and speak the truth, hoping to combat the comforting lies and self-dealing spin that belch back from social media.

The privilege and responsibility of my job weigh on me in times like this. As stories pour out, questions pour in, and as a journalist, I seek answers. I do my best to help viewers navigate our swiftly changing world. The platform I've built over the course of my long career grants me the privilege and tasks me with the responsibility of speaking to millions of people on a daily basis. I take it seriously. I try to amplify the right voices, even when they disagree with me. I want to hear from good troublemakers like

John Lewis and disruptors like Colin Kaepernick. This is not the time for diffidence, modesty, or "after you, my dear Gaston" propriety. It's time to have a point of view, not just an opinion.

This is a moment, to be sure, but it's not an island; it's part of the continuum that begins every time we say *now*, a timeline reinvented by each breath, each blink, each word out of your mouth. If there is a message in this moment, it is a clarion call from our collective future, begging us: *Don't screw this up*. I intend to step up, stay visible, and stand on the right side of history without faltering.

I challenge you to do the same.

The true agents of change in this moment will be those who think of themselves as one of the many. There's an urgent cry rising up from street corners and social media, voices from outside the establishment, all of whom contribute some element of insight, sorrow, humor, or pathos to the evolving colloquy. Our greatest source of bold idealism is our young people, for they are the ones with the most at stake, and their fresh awakening to this reality has given them a backbone we haven't seen in the establishment lately. These children do not simply march in the footsteps of John Lewis, Martin Luther King, Harry Belafonte, or Lena Horne, who were in their twenties and thirties when they started shaking things up. No, our young people have their own trail to blaze and a totally new way of blazing it. We'll do well to listen. I'm asking you to open your mind and allow space for potentially uncomfortable ideas.

In the tradition of James Baldwin, this book is an open letter to my nieces and grand-nephews. These children Tim and I love are Black and White, and we are there for every one of them unconditionally. We plan to walk with them—and with our own children someday—through Azurest, a neighborhood that, according to all edicts of the day, was not allowed to exist. But there it stands, exemplifying a place, a time, and a way of life that was grappled into being by the grit and industry of ruthlessly marginalized people. The rooftops of Azurest are soaring, sturdily trussed, watertight evidence that change is not only possible, it is inevitable, and we must either embody and fight for the evolved society we long to live in, or live in the unsustainable, dry-rotting society engineered by those who would have us die with their knees on our necks.

I will not pretend to have all the answers. I'm deeply suspicious of anyone who says they do. Now, more than ever, we must be skeptical of absolutes that polarize us. We must be steely of soul, tolerating no what-about-ism, thoughts'n'prayers pandering, or mealy-mouthed kumbaya. We must reject puritans of all stripes and welcome disagreement.

Let's leave behind the circular, choir-preaching conversations in which everyone agrees. No progress has ever been made in the timorous pursuit of getting back to normal or pleasing all of the people all of the time. I consider it an honor when someone thinks highly enough of my opinion to be pissed off by it. That's fine. Jesus said the truth would set you free; he never said you had to like it. Several years of social media scathing has endowed me with the thick skin and sturdy shoulders of an armadillo. I'm grateful to be having this conversation in an era of unprecedented connectedness.

<hr />

"If the word *integration* means anything," Baldwin wrote to his nephew, "this is what it means: that we, with love, shall force our brothers to see themselves as they are, to cease fleeing from reality and begin to change it. For this is your home, my friend, do not be driven from it...You come from a long line of great poets, some of the greatest poets since Homer. One of them said, *'The very time I thought I was lost, My dungeon shook and my chains fell off.'*"

In 2020, our dungeon shook. We watched, astonished, as our societal chains fell. Now comes the hard part: We have to sit down now—*sit down,* on the ground, right now—to speak real truth to each other and work this damn thing out.

Black brothers and sisters: We must swallow our righteous wrath, making it clear that we will do our best to forgive, though we dare not ever forget.

White brothers and sisters: I challenge you to overcome your uncertainty and allow yourselves to be schooled—without expecting Black people to school you.

Folks of all races, ages, and persuasions will have to turn toward those with whom we disagree, those who fear change, and we must challenge ourselves to listen to their concerns before we attempt to exorcise their dread.

We must summon the courage to love people who infuriate us, because we love the world we share more than we hate the ignorance and apprehension that shackle those people to an irredeemable past. We must offer them a way to lay down that burden and get shed of that shame—at last, at long last—because if they miss this singular moment, if this unique opportunity for redemption passes them by, we will meet them again on some leafy spring morning not far down the road. And on that day, you better believe, they'll have a bigger dog.

2

We Didn't Get Here by Accident

Louisiana sticks to you. Thick, subtropical humidity sticks to your skin. The Cajun and Creole cuisine sticks to your insides, making you feel satisfied and slow. Layers of antiquity cling to the gnarled oaks and mossy bridge abutments. The ever-present past injects itself everywhere, like the weeds that persist between the rotting railroad ties. History hangs just within earshot, like the ambient whine of the cicadas. For thousands of years, prehistoric people hunted and gathered all up and down the muddy riverbanks of the Mississippi. They established thriving urban centers and trade routes, navigating swamps filled with alligators, cypress knees, and the occasional orchid.

The Mississippian culture evolved concurrent with Europe's Middle Ages. Early Muskogean people engineered and built enormous mounds to raise their sacred sites and family homes above the reach of floodwaters. Louisiana reclines close to the earth, spooning with her great love, the Mississippi; miles from the coast, swales dip down below sea level, like a stealthy hand under the covers. Every spring, the Mississippi swells with runoff from the melting snow up north, and floodwaters overwhelm everything in the river's drunken path. The lowland areas are inundated, and when the water recedes, lush grass and palmy undergrowth proliferate: a million kinds of green, teeming with lizards, water birds, and bugs the size of chicken wings.

The Spanish arrived in the early 1500s; they didn't stay, but the lingering effects of disease and greed shadowed the native population. In 1698, a French expedition making its way up the Mississippi noted a thirty-foot pole, painted with crimson pigment from the bloodroot plant and decorated with fish bones. This *bâton rouge* (French for "red stick") had been posted to mark the boundary between two tribal territories. French folks settled nearby, joined by hearty Cajuns, French-speaking people driven out of Canada by the British. *Voilà!* Baton Rouge became a thing.

In 1803, the United States paid France $15 million (about $18 per square mile) for a 530-million-acre wedge right in the middle of North America. (Again: *Breathe,*

Tim, breathe.) This is called the Louisiana Purchase when we learn about it in school, but that's like saying I "purchased" the Chrysler Building from you for fifty bucks. The people who actually own the Chrysler Building would not be down with that. So the Louisiana "Purchase" is more like me paying you fifty bucks to step out of the way while I go into the Chrysler Building, shove the current residents down an elevator shaft, and gut the place like an HGTV flip house.

The most cost-conscious way to cultivate this stolen land was, of course, stolen labor. According to statistics kept by Whitney Plantation, there were ten Africans in Louisiana in 1712. Ten years later, there were 170. By the end of the century, twenty thousand enslaved Africans abducted from Senegambia, Benin, and Biafra labored on Louisiana's farms and plantations. Many intermarried with Indigenous people, and their offspring labored alongside them. Essential to the production of valuable cash crops, mainly indigo and sugarcane, several generations of Black laborers were branded, mutilated, and flogged into submission, while plantation owners and their families amassed huge fortunes and gained political influence.

In January 1811, on the swath of land between Baton Rouge and New Orleans known as the German Coast,

Charles Deslondes—a 31-year-old overseer, born to a Black enslaved mother, fathered by an unknown White man—organized and led what would be the largest slave uprising in United States history. Two Black slaves, Quamana and Kook, worked with Deslondes to rally support through a secret communications network that used dances, drums, and nonverbal signals to convey messages between enslaved people at the surrounding plantations.

Inspired by stories of the French Revolution and the success of a recent uprising in Haiti, twenty-five men set out late at night in the pouring rain, with dozens more soon joining their ranks, following the levees along the east bank of the Mississippi. They marched in formation, many wearing pilfered military uniforms. As dozens became hundreds, Deslondes, Kook, and Quamana organized the marchers in subunits, each with a leader on horseback. Recorded accounts are confused and biased, but it's undisputed that by the following day, several hundred slaves had joined the uprising, carrying flags, marching to the beat of drums, armed with hammers, hand tools, and the cane knives they used for harvesting sugar.

Their objective was nothing less than freedom; they intended to establish an autonomous society for themselves and their children in a region near New Orleans where a large number of freed Black people were living. They knew what would happen if the rebellion failed. It's impossible to overstate the raw courage of every person who took their place in the march.

Several plantation buildings were burned and two White people were killed as the rebels marched more than twenty miles, from present-day LaPlace to St. Rose. The planters summoned militia groups that swarmed up from New Orleans and down from Baton Rouge, armed with guns and bayonets. The German Coast Uprising was swiftly, savagely put down. At least sixty-six of those who fled were killed in the lopsided battle, and many others died uncounted, shrugged off as collateral damage. Sixteen were interrogated and hanged by a tribunal of angry plantation owners. Some broke under torture and named names, hoping to save themselves, but Kook and Quamana remained silent, defying their captors to the bitter end.

Deslondes was brought down by dogs and made an example. His captors cut off his hands and put them on display. They shot him in one leg and then the other, to shatter the bones so he couldn't run. As he bled, they bundled him in straw and set him on fire. They wanted the marchers to hear him screaming as he burned to death.

According to tribunal records, the planters ordered that "as a terrible example to all who would disturb the public tranquility in the future," the dead should be decapitated and the heads posted on pikes atop the levees. Scores of rotting heads—varying accounts place the number between sixty and one hundred—were displayed in a gruesome spectacle that extended mile after mile along the riverbank. To the modern imagination, this sounds like some over-the-top *Game of Thrones* moment or a vision straight out of ancient Rome, when the roads in and out of the city were lined with crucifixions, sometimes of many hundreds of victims. But this was America in the not-so-distant past. This was the "gallant South" celebrated in the lilting parlor melodies of Stephen Foster: *Camptown ladies sing dis song, doo-dah, doo-dah! Beautiful dreamer, awake unto me. Long may the daisies dance the field.* This is the South of *Gone with the Wind*—Twelve Oaks and Tara and all the magnolia-shaded plantations.

The bloody pikes stood in grim counterpoint to the original *bâton rouge,* marking a boundary of a different sort, voicing with ruthless clarity a pointed warning for any Black person who dared to imagine anything that looked like freedom: *This is as far as you go.*

Crows feasted and grew fat. Black survivors of the march, along with those who were too old or young or weak to attempt it, passed by the decaying remains of their loved ones as they returned to the fields of sugarcane and indigo. The White planters and their families returned to their tranquility. Journalists wrote very little about these events at the time—or ever. The first full account seems to be a lengthy article written by local historian and slaveowner Charles Gayarré in 1866, citing the incident as a laudable example of White supremacy.

Gayarré praised the decisive action taken by the plantation owners, who were sorely outnumbered by their Black slaves, and marveled at the ineptitude of the "misguided negroes" who had killed only two White people and burned a few buildings when they could have killed many more and laid waste to everything in their path. To him and his ilk, freedom and autonomy were flaccid aspirations when compared with the grand ambition of domination by brute force. Gayarré underscored the abiding hope and fear of White supremacists, writing that the Black rebels "had been deluded into this foolish attempt at gaining a position in society, which, for the welfare of their own race, will ever be denied to it in the Southern States of North America, as long as their White population is not annihilated or subjugated."

White supremacists—active and passive, present and past—would like to pretend their credo is "Give me liberty or give me death," when in fact their abiding doctrine is "Give me what I want or I'll kill you." The specificity of their intention could not be more apparent. On the surface, their pragmatic goal was to use Black bodies as machinery for the economy. But there was something deeper, something diabolical, that's more difficult to explain. What sort of orgy mentality leads "normal" men to engage in a group effort as deranged as the ritualistic torture and murder of Charles Deslondes and the casual acceptance of bloody, rotting heads being displayed on a public thoroughfare? I ask over and over, *Who the hell does that?* And who the hell *ignores* that?

I also wonder how this history impacts events unfolding in the present. Who could perpetrate such a spiritually diseased act and then go on to shape a psychologically healthy society? Who could endure that level of trauma and go on with their life undamaged? Who witnesses atrocity of that caliber and walks away unchanged?

I'll tell you who: *No one. Ever.*

It sticks.

I spent my early childhood in Port Allen, a suburb across the river from downtown Baton Rouge, less than fifty miles from the area where the German Coast Uprising took place. Sugar was still the economic backbone of the region. I remember the smell of burnt sugar in the air, warm and cloying, like the smell of toasted marshmallows, whenever the sugar factory was in full steam. I played with my sisters, Leisa and Yma, on two old sugarcane trucks that were parked on my grandparents' property.

My father, Wilmon Richardson, was an attorney in Baton Rouge. Long story short, he was Black Perry Mason, and my mom, Katherine, was Black Della Street.

They never married, but they were devoted to each other, and I had a great relationship with my father. I was nine years old when he died from complications of diabetes. We were remodeling our house, and he stepped on a nail. It became infected, and he had to have his toe amputated. But that didn't heal, so he had to have his foot amputated. And then they took his leg right up to his knee. Eventually a blood clot reached his heart, and he died.

My mother eventually married, and I had a good relationship with my stepfather as well. There was no lack of love and connection in my family, and I think that's because of—not in spite of—our complex history of unorthodox relationships. I come from a long line of people who did what they had to do to live, led by love rather than standard protocol. We've always had our ways.

"*Waaaays*," my mom and sisters like to say, exchanging a knowing look.

It's part of our secret language, my family's own lexicon of drums, dances, and nonverbal signals. I no longer wonder where it comes from, because not long ago I learned that Catherine Woods, my third great-grandmother, was the granddaughter of a Black man abducted from Africa and sold into slavery on a Louisiana plantation about the time of the Louisiana Purchase, just a few years before the German Coast Uprising. His name and the date of his death are unknown, as is much of Black history, but the Uprising encompassed so much of this region, I can't dismiss the possibility that he may have marched with Kook and Quamana—that he might have died with them. At the very least, he would have heard about the rebellion and witnessed its horrific aftermath.

The particulars of my African lineage came to me as part of a CNN special in which I explored my ancestry with family historian Michelle Ercanbrack from Ancestry .com. This was an emotional journey I could not have made without my mom. We flew together to what is now called the Slave Coast in Ghana and, retracing the footsteps of our unnamed African forefather, visited Cape Coast Castle, a grand citadel where African abductees were imprisoned and held before transport to thriving slave markets in the Americas.

On the flight to Africa, Mom and I bantered back and forth, the way we always do.

"Mom, don't take pictures of the food."

"I like how they give you the sleep mask in the first-class kit."

"What was the name of that restaurant with the alligator tacos?"

That kind of thing. Neither of us was prepared for the gravity of what we were about to experience. We continued like tourists (make that *American* tourists) who expect all the comforts of home to be close at hand while we ogle things you can't see in Louisiana. We marveled at the matchless cerulean sky and were touched by the joy and generosity of the people. We ate food that was just foreign enough to flavor the experience.

Driving to the castle, we saw children playing in the water with not a stitch of clothes on. A fresh ocean breeze carried their voices, all unfiltered joy and enviable freedom. Mom and I laughed, but I felt a fleeting shadow of sadness.

"I can't imagine feeling so comfortable in my own skin as a kid," I said, and part of me wondered, *Could that have been me? If my ancestor hadn't been taken, would I have been as free and fearless as they are?*

My life has been blessed with love and opportunity, but let's be real: I grew up gay and Black in the South in the 1970s. My childhood was also marred by a period of sexual abuse (by a neighbor, not a family member), so I was, in part, shaped by the trauma of that experience and the daily task of survivorship. For years, I was cocooned in a formative shame that came with the secret, the degraded sense of self that results when one's body is criminally commandeered and violated by another. That sort of injury tends to fester, killing by inches, taking a toe, and then a foot, and then a leg. I survived it, but it took something from me.

As a kid, I felt trapped in what I call the "Black box": a finite parameter of low expectations imposed on Black children, on Black potential, on Black possibility—on Black *life*. I was aware of the Black box from the time I was aware of my own hands, so it came as no surprise to me in high school when White parents fussed about "some Black kid" (me) being elected class president. As a student of journalism at Louisiana State University, I was unfazed when a professor told me, "I don't know why you're here. You're not going to make it in this business."

The Black box is built on old business and buttressed by foregone conclusions that constantly, quietly inject racism and White supremacy into the very fiber of American discourse.

Fun Fact: That little song you hear played by an ice cream truck—you know, the one that kinda sounds like "Turkey in the Straw"—yeah, that song is actually called "Nigger Love a Watermelon Ha! Ha! Ha!"

I kid you not. Google it. That's what that is.

Whether we admit it or not, the subtle presence of racism and White supremacy plays like that innocuous little ditty on endless repeat up and down every street in every town in the United States of America. Preconceptions and prejudices are so deeply ingrained, they don't even register, but we feel it. We respond exactly as we've been programmed to respond. Tell me you don't hear that song and start searching your pockets for a dollar.

It's easy to condemn White supremacy when it's writ large in the form of Confederate monuments and church-burning; it's harder to push back against microaggressions and small acts of discrimination that tumble by in a babbling brook of subconscious influences.

Watching the children scuffle and romp in the waves on the coast of Africa, I wondered aloud, "What would it be like to grow up without that undermining soundtrack in your head?"

"What would it be like to grow up without air conditioning?" Mom countered.

The heat was palpable in the flagstone courtyard at Cape Coast Castle, where we met our tour guide, Esso. The castle itself stands, impervious to the passage of time, gleaming white on a high curtain of rock that shears up from a cobalt-blue ocean. On the ramparts, an imposing row of iron cannons juts out, aimed at the open water. Two tall bastions flank the iron sea gate. Inside, the upper stories once housed luxurious accommodations, offices, and kitchens. Below are the dungeons—one for males, another for females—connected by a network of dank, tomblike tunnels. The entrance is like the mouth of some medieval hell. Descending into it, I felt cold sweat trickle down my spine.

Leading us through the catacombs, Esso pointed out the gully in the floor that vented feces and urine of up to a thousand people at a time for an average of three months.

"This was a dungeon for the troublemakers," he said, "those who were instigating violence. They were held here in chains, so you see the holes in the wall."

I didn't want to think about what it would mean to spend months shackled there in utter darkness. I kept looking for any crevice for light to come in, any crawlspace through which one might escape, but there was none. A person would die here or be dragged out to die on a slave ship or, at best, to die in slavery. Esso led us through another narrow passage to a wooden door. He pointed out a sign above it: *Door of No Return.*

"What you are standing before now is a shrine," said Esso. "Through this door, they left behind the known for the unknown. Behind this wall, there was a tunnel through which the captives were led to the exits."

"To get to the ships," Mom said.

"Yes, to get on the boats and into the ships," said Esso. "Now the walls are dedicated to the souls of our ancestors."

We lit a candle for the memory of our forefather and all the spirits who remained within these walls. In the light of the small bright flame, I saw tears on my mother's face. I pulled her into my arms and kissed the top of her head.

"We're survivors," I said.

Esso pushed the door open, and we passed through it, into blinding sunlight. It was almost unbearable in

46

contrast to the overwhelming gloom. On the other side of the door was another sign: *Door of Return.*

"On behalf of the government and people of this country," said Esso, "it's my pleasure to welcome you back."

When Barack Obama and his family passed through this same doorway in 2009, he said the castle reminded him of Buchenwald. He noted the ironic presence of a church directly over the troublemakers' dungeon, a reminder of how comfortably good and evil are able to coexist in the minds of piously complicit bystanders.

Obama said, "I think it was particularly important for Malia and Sasha, who are growing up in such a blessed way, to be reminded that history can take very cruel turns, and hopefully, one of the things that was imparted to them during this trip is their sense of obligation to fight oppression and cruelty wherever it appears, and that any group of people who are degrading another group of people have to be fought against with whatever tools we have available to us."

Whatever tools, the man said. Once it was hammers and cane knives; now it's voices and votes.

Mom was quiet on the long drive back to our hotel in the city. I'd been to Africa before, but she didn't know what to expect. The topography was beautiful—the water, the hills—but she wasn't prepared for the level of poverty she saw.

I squeezed her hand and said, "You okay, Mom?"

She nodded, but I could see she was blinking back tears.

"I could not have made this trip without you," I told her. "I'm so glad I got to share this with you."

"You've shown me so much of the world," she said, "taken me places I never imagined going. I've had experiences I never thought I'd have. You did that for me. I'm just so proud of you."

I told her how grateful I was for everything she'd given me and how glad I was to share all of it with her—the good times and the difficult. Now we were both crying, hugging it out. It meant a lot to me. There was a time when I was afraid she would be disappointed in me, maybe even disown me, if she knew the truth about who I am. Her gay son. I was haunted by the idea that my mere presence would be a source of heartache for her. I could not have been more mistaken. When I finally opened up to her, came out and owned it all, she was there for me with nothing but love, acceptance, and respect.

Mom and I were emotionally and physically exhausted by the time we got back to our hotel, still jet-lagged and longing for sleep, yet we didn't want the day to end.

"Let's go have a drink," I said, and she was all for it. We found a spot overlooking the ocean and shared a bottle of wine as dusk disappeared and stars emerged in the night sky.

"I have to confess something," said Mom. "I'm glad we came, but I'm glad I don't live here. I don't know how to make sense of it. The way our family was taken from this place—it's wrong. It's ugly. It's—I don't know. There aren't words to describe what that is. Our people left here in the worst possible conditions, through the dungeon and the darkness, put on that ship. But we flew here. First class. It was awesome. And we brought part of them back with us. What a statement that is about who we've become. What a testament to the power of God."

People, let's take a moment to unpack that profound observation.

We didn't get here by accident. The moment in which we find ourselves, as a nation and as individuals, was purposefully contrived by people whose agenda had nothing to do with creating a better world. They designed an unscrupulous economic system that built family fortunes by stripping men, women, and children of their humanity. They didn't go off half-cocked; everything they did, they did with the malicious intent and stone-cold forethought required to bundle a man in straw before setting him on fire. They developed sickeningly precise methods that radically modified behavior, altered mindsets, and instilled a lasting gestalt that reflects their values to this day.

We must undo all that, designing a new system and instilling a changed gestalt, from a higher place. Newton's Third Law states: "For every action, there is an equal and opposite reaction." The economic imperative of our purpose must be equal and opposite to the economic imperative of their purpose. The specificity of our methods must be equal and opposite to the specificity of their methods. The decisiveness of our action must be equal and opposite to the decisiveness of their action. Where they were relentlessly cruel, we must be relentlessly kind. Where they were consumed with self-interest, we must be consumed with community and global responsibility. Let our progression juxtapose their regression. Let our decency neutralize their barbarism. We can and must be the blinding sunlight that dispels their utter darkness.

Mom and I sat by the sea talking until late that night. We shed a lot of tears. We'd committed to do this CNN special, thinking, *Hey, that'll be cool.* It cut a lot deeper than either of us expected, and we still had a long way to go.

The following week, Michelle Ercanbrack met us in Louisiana to discuss our family's place in the African American diaspora. We walked around Cinclare Plantation, the abandoned sugarcane mill where my great-grandmother Catherine Jackson worked when she was young. The plant's White overseer, Harry Rivault, was my great-grandfather. We have no way of knowing the true nature of their relationship, but we were presented with compelling evidence that they loved each other in the only way that worked at the time.

Growing up, my mother had heard a story that Catherine died in childbirth when Mame was born.

"Harry Rivault wanted to take her and raise her," said Mom, "but her grandparents came and got her."

As we walked through Managers Row, the pleasant Edwardian neighborhood where the company housed the higher-ups, I wondered what it would have been like for Mame to grow up there, the only Black child in a White neighborhood at a time when many of the mill workers were Black folks born into slavery before the Civil War. Harry Rivault lived there with his wife, Odell, but they never had children. According to the coroner's report, when Harry was 56 years old, he placed a 12-gauge shotgun against his head and pulled the trigger.

I wish I'd asked Mame what she knew about her father. She never talked about him. We don't know how he was involved in her life and were stunned when Michelle told us that before he died, Harry Rivault bought Mame a house.

"I never knew that." Mom shook her head, taking it in. "My mom said she saved the money to buy it, and she never worked, so we always wondered."

I received this information along with the acrid smell of burnt sugarcane that still lingers in the heavy summer air. Little remains of the massive machinery that once powered Cinclare Plantation. The old mill shut down and was parted out years ago. The rusted gears and pulleys have been scattered to architectural salvage yards. People incorporate bits and pieces in trendy décor and upscale loft apartments. A touch of steampunk. A whiff of industrial irony. The ghosts have been carefully removed with steel wool and astringent cleaner. There is no trace of the girl who died in childbirth or the man who put a gun to his head. Everything about their lives is obsolete.

But here's the thing: the man tried. Clearly, he wanted to do right by a woman he apparently loved and a daughter for whom he felt responsible. The stifling atmosphere of turn-of-the-century Louisiana left him with very few options, and the jarring details of his death left me with a thousand questions.

Truth is, there's darkness beneath the floorboards of Louisiana. Between the layers of lush vegetation, beyond the beautiful idiosyncrasy, there lurks a shadow of shame and regret. I'd always sensed that and assumed it was about me; now I was beginning to see the big picture. As a Black man with White heritage, I embody both the struggle for survival and the hope of reconciliation. This makes me what we all are, each in our own way, each of us the immutable consequence of our own unique journey: *American.*

What we are in our hearts, we will be as a nation, and what we choose to be now, as a nation, will be written above our own gates of no return.

3

My Lord, What a Mourning When the Stars Begin to Fall

My sister Leisa was a mainstay in my life from my earliest memories. She was the oldest, followed two years later by my sister Yma. I came along five years after that, the baby of the family, and I won't lie, they doted on me. Leisa was old enough to be that little lieutenant caregiver who helped Mame while Mom was at work. Leisa's oldest was born a few weeks after I graduated high school, and Leisa let me name her Ashleigh, a popular baby name elevated with a spelling twist.

Whenever Leisa was away, training or on duty as a member of the Army Reserve, I stepped up to care for baby Ashleigh. Her dad dropped her off on his way to work, and I took my little chickadee to class with me at LSU, toting her in the car-seat carrier with a diaper bag full of pacifying snacks and activities along with my freshman textbooks. When Ashleigh was big enough, I taught her to swim, just as Leisa and Yma had taught me, and after Ashleigh's son Trushaad was born, I taught him, too. That's how we do in our family, as most Black families do. Roles shift and expand to cover changing needs. You're always on deck for the people you love, and they're always on deck for you.

Leisa taught me how to drive and how to dress and impressed upon me the value of a dollar. She was supportive and incredibly proud of me as I worked my way through school and up the ranks to become an anchor at CNN. In 2018, I was anchoring *CNN Tonight,* and Leisa had literally worn the letters off her CNN tee shirt.

I was at work when Yma called to tell me that Leisa had drowned in the lake near her home.

This information sank in with the visceral astonishment you feel when stepping on a nail. Pain, instantaneous and all-encompassing, travels the axis of your body. Shock constricts your throat and leaves a baffled white noise in your brain. You go to autopilot, ask pertinent questions, assimilate answers. Words fall out of your mouth like twisted metal and broken cinder block. Wreckage words.

Time and emotion are reduced to shrapnel. Those ninety seconds are like eons separating you from whatever life you expected to lead when you stepped out of the shower that morning. This is how abstraction—*Black Lives Matter*—becomes real: a life that was intertwined with your life, a death that feels like a part of you has died.

Leisa was dead. But Leisa was Leisa and therefore could not be dead, because Leisa does not drown in a damn lake behind her house six years short of Social Security; my sister is a force of nature with all the tensile confidence of a coiled spring. She must be alive, because I need her. The cacophony of denial in my head gave way to the rhythm of Yma's sobbing. My office was quiet except for that sound from the phone, like the sound of a faraway bird, and I became quiet, too.

My first unclouded thought was for Mom. After hanging up with Yma, I called her.

"Don," she said, "Leisa is dead." I discerned a few broken words—*saw her body…paramedics…they took her*—and then her throaty voice was lost to a deep, heart-wrenching wail that cascaded into uncontrollable weeping. Neither of us remembers much about the call. We don't want to remember that fraught hour before composure came, pragmatic and fixed, like the steel pins and plaster cast that stabilize a shattered bone. Sitting stiffly in my office chair, I called Ashleigh and her sisters and said, "I'm coming home."

I work with an amazing team of compassionate, detail-oriented people at CNN. Within minutes, they had surrounded me, triaged the show situation, and made travel arrangements. My boss, Jeff Zucker, came to sit with me and didn't leave until I was in a car on my way to the airport. The driver was on two wheels all the way. I made it just in time to catch the last flight to New Orleans. I rented a car, drove to Baton Rouge, and picked up Yma.

We got to Mom's house at two in the morning. The streets were empty, all the houses dark, windows curtained like downcast eyes. It felt oddly appropriate. It was customary in Victorian times to spread straw on the street in front of a home of a grieving family to muffle the sound of horses and carriages passing by. There's such empathy in that gesture, this recognition that we are hypersensitized and made vulnerable by loss. I'm not sure I could have borne harsh daylight and diurnal bustle at that moment. Yma and I sat quietly with Mom as we called Leisa's daughters.

Competing riptides of emotion and necessity carried us through the following days. Arrangements. Notifications. All manner of paperwork none of us had imagined would be necessary so soon. Too soon. Mom paced and talked nonstop, wired with a weird frenetic energy, trying to fill the space where Leisa should have been. She couldn't stop dwelling on their last conversation.

"You deserve some time to yourself," Mom had told Leisa. "You should get out and go fishing."

That was their thing. They'd been fishing together since Leisa was little. They both had lakeshore homes. They compared catches and shared animated stories of the ones that got away. I tried to tell her, "Mom, let it go," but she kept pacing and chattering, examining and reexamining every day on every wooden dock of Leisa's life, every cast of the lure, every line arcing out over that dark water, questioning her unwitting role in this catastrophic twist of fate.

We waited for the autopsy, hoping for some explanation—embolism, aneurysm, anything that might have caused her to fall or make her incapable of swimming—but there was nothing beyond the vague police report assumption that she had "tripped" and her death "appeared accidental." There was no foul play suspected, but there was no fair play either. The baffling senselessness of my sister's death cast a shadow on every family conversation from which she was now and forever absent.

My journalist brain needled me at night. *How? Why? Why? How?* In the absence of answers, my mother blamed herself. People who didn't know Leisa fell into a natural tendency to fill the answer vacuum with cautionary tales ("You should never go out on the water alone") or bias-based assumptions ("Oh, she must have been drinking"). People naturally go there, because the only alternative is the potentially paralyzing realization that we live in a chaotic universe where terrible things sometimes happen to wonderful people for no damn reason. If we're capable of love, we're vulnerable to loss, and it's painful to be reminded of that.

When the story broke on Page Six and other media shared on Facebook, thousands of kind condolences were posted in response. Comment threads were quickly infected with the inevitable troll scat about CNN being "fake news" and me being "Satan's prophet," but overwhelmingly, people were on the side of decency, compassion, and respect for my family's privacy. My first night back on the air, I thanked the long list of folks who'd extended encouragement to me and my family, including Sean Hannity, Megyn Kelly, and a few other people with whom I vocally, vehemently disagree on a regular basis.

"There's so much conflict right now," I said. "I think it's important for all Americans to know that something like this tends to bring out the best in people — even some of my competitors and people I have raging arguments with on television. You think we hate each other, but we don't."

After my sister's funeral, I returned to work, feeling capable but raw, grateful for the intensity of this job that requires my full focus and forces me to put one foot in front of the other, twenty-six hours a day. I rolled out of bed at dark-thirty in the morning and set my eyes on the floor, watching my feet as I walked, as if the world beneath me might disintegrate at any moment. I counted my steps from front door to car door to office door to studio. I prepped for the show, did the show, and then counted my steps from studio to office door to car door to front door, and then a few hours later, I rolled out to do it again.

Loss changes us, but it takes time to discern the true depth and breadth of this shift in paradigm. I always considered myself a "glass-half-full" sort of person, but between the 2016 election cycle and the loss of Leisa in January 2018, I felt my innate hopefulness diminish. Headlines scrolled by, leaving me half-empty.

Warren Buffett confirmed that Trump's "Tax Cut and Jobs Act" had gifted multinational conglomerate Berkshire Hathaway a sweet $29 billion.

MIT determined that the average Uber driver made $3.37/hour.

KFC was toying with the rollout of edible coffee cups lined with white chocolate.

Black Lives Matter protesters were marching in California and New York, decrying the latest tragedy. Two Sacramento police officers, following up on a 911 call about someone breaking car windows, saw 22-year-old Stephon Clark in his grandmother's backyard, thought his cell phone looked like a gun, and unloaded ten rounds each, striking him twenty times—an astonishing feat of marksmanship, considering how it was too dark to tell the difference between a cell phone and a gun.

Body-cam footage released in the wake of the protests

showed that while Stephon lay bleeding to death, the officers waited for backup, occasionally shouting at him to show his hands. Eventually they turned over Stephon's lifeless body and saw the cell phone.

"Fuck," said the officer. Moments later, they muted the mics on their body cams.

The officers were put on paid administrative leave, and the usual band of BLM protesters took to the streets. They stormed a Sacramento city council meeting with Stephon's brother, Stevante Clark, who danced, shrieked himself hoarse, and bounded up onto the dais in front of the startled mayor of Sacramento—a moment that was designed to go viral.

For the next several days, focus swerved away from Stephon's bullet-riddled body to Stevante's manic, wildly aggrieved antics, which many people found unseemly. To me, Stevante seemed like an intelligent, creative, passionately well-intentioned young man, and I didn't think his behavior was all that firestorm-worthy. I was more offended by the way so many people, Black and White, felt the need to quibble over his behavior, rather than scrutinize the outrageous circumstances of Stephon's death or, God forbid, ponder the four hundred years of outrageous abuse, torture, rape, murder, and disenfranchisement of Black people in the United States.

In terms of story coverage, media attention to my sister's death was based on the public's passing curiosity about the private lives of celebrities. ("Oh! Apparently, this talking head has a heart that can actually be broken. Who knew?") The story of Stephon Clark's death was part of a much larger story that never seems to get any attention until the bleeding body of a Black person headlines the show. Think about it in the context of everything from #OscarsSoWhite to your American history textbook: When are Black people seen and Black voices heard? Who's paying attention if we're not looting, dying, or putting on a show?

When that toxic brand of attention rivets suddenly on a Black family in grief, racist trolls are always at the ready, mouths watering, eager to pounce. The denialists are prepared with a long list of "what abouts" that can be used to assiduously deconstruct the scenario from every angle until they find a way—*aneurysm, embolism, anything*—that makes it possible for them to blame the victim, shame the family, dismiss protesters out of hand, and boil egregious systemic issues down to bad apples and tragic mishaps. Those who fight indefatigably for this cause, day in and day out, must be exhausted by the idea of having to triage amateurs and do the spin control it takes to get their message out. So when Stevante came along and kicked the hornet's nest of public opinion, he was guaranteed to get it from all sides.

Comment-section spectators spared no venom, and there were some obvious looks of consternation at Stephon's wake, where Stevante mugged and postured, draped his arms around Al Sharpton's neck, and tried to bogart the mic while his sister, Shai'Ellesse Works, spoke briefly about how smart Stephon was, how he took all honors classes at a Sacramento charter school. She'd helped him with his homework; he'd teased her about being less fun than their grandmother.

"I just wanted to give you guys a good memory," she said. "I just wanted to let you know he was an amazing child. He was smart beyond smart."

Al Sharpton firmly pushed the mic away from Stevante and toward Shai'Ellesse, but later, the Rev laid it down for any "uppity, bourgeois, proper folk" who felt authorized to judge Stevante and the protesters, online and off: "You don't tell people in pain how to handle their pain. You don't tell people, when you kill their loved one, how to grieve...It's time for preachers to come outta the pulpit. It's time for politicians to come outta the office. It's time for us to go down and stop this madness. Some reporter said to me about how this brother and others stopped cars. They stopped this young man's *life!* [Protesters] didn't shoot at anybody twenty times. They've not been violent. They're asking for *you* to stop being violent to *them!*"

I wanted Stephon's story to be heard, and I was told Stevante wanted to talk to me, so that evening, after the wake, we had him on the show. At the start of the segment,

I said, "First, let me express, again, my sympathy here. How's your family holding up? How are you holding up?"

Stevante tapped a sharp *ping!* on a little bell—like the little service bell you'd tap at a dry cleaner's—and then posed, glaring at the camera. I allowed an open moment before asking, "What does that mean?"

"Next question."

"Okay..."

I immediately realized that this was not going to be cool. He wasn't ready. There's never a time when I'm about exploiting a family's grief; I want to talk to people when it's cathartic, constructive, and healthy for them to talk to me. I was keenly aware of that obligation at this moment, just a few weeks after my sister's death, when I myself was still raw and bereft. I felt a protective surge of brotherly concern for this young guy whose anguish was a burden I knew.

I said, "Obviously, you are in grief right now, and listen—"

"I'm not in grief."

"All right..."

"We haven't slept," he said. "We haven't ate. The media keeps following us everywhere we go. The only person that got the message—and that was just before we came on the air—was the mayor. He has called me, and he said he's going to help us build the library and the recreational center that's twenty-four hours..."

His voice choked up, but his eyes were dry. I couldn't tell if it was genuine emotion or an attempt at the old James Brown feint. Someone off camera said something to him, and Stevante turned to retort, "*I am!* I am. Okay? I am."

"So the mayor has said he's going to help you build a library?" I said, trying to nudge him back on track, but the interview quickly went off the rails, and that's a no-win situation. For a jumbled minute or so, I tried to bring attention back to Stephon and the message of the protests while Stevante talked over me, spiraling, agitated, exuding a darker, angrier version of that frenetic energy I'd seen in my mother the night Leisa died. It was that same aching need to fill a fathomless void, but within my mother, there is a seasoned core of strength and self-awareness. In Stevante, I sensed only the turbid rage of a young man who's probably been made to feel invisible his entire life. Now the all-seeing public eye had turned on him in a moment driven by sorrow, two-wheeling adrenaline, and naked frustration.

"What the media does—they wait until a loved one dies," he said. "They find out it's a tragedy. They swarm that person. They put them in grief. They ruin their lives. *Forever.* Their lives are never the same."

"If the—"

"Don Lemon! *Don Lemon!* Let me talk to my people,

okay? You Black. I'm Black. Let's be Black now. Don't you do that now, Don Lemon."

"Well, I just want to tell you—"

"Don't start!"

"The media—listen—"

"*Hold on hold on hold on*—I'm not blaming the media. I'm not blaming. But the way you guys treat us, you guys—I stopped calling up. We have—how many phones do we have in the family? Seven? Eight?"

"Listen," I said, "I have to manage the time here so that we can get something out of this interview, because a lot of people are watching, and through the media, whether you like it or not, your brother's story will be told. The media is giving you a platform. Tell me about your brother, please."

"We love Stephon—*I am*," he snarled at whoever was talking to him offstage, and then he struck a pose for the camera, teeth clenched, lip curled. "Don Lemon, say his name, Don Lemon. *Say. His. Name.*"

The whole thing felt very theatrical and disconcerting. My goal was to end it gracefully before he made himself any more vulnerable.

"Stevante, listen. You're in grief..."

He threw his arms wide. "He's not going to say his name!"

"You're in grief. I'm sorry for that."

He talked over me. "We'll never do CNN! You used—our name—you—you sent our driver late. That's messed up."

"I know how it is," I said. "I just recently lost my sister as well."

I hadn't intended to share that. I believe a journalist should bring the empathy and understanding they gain from life experiences without injecting their personal narrative into the story of the moment. But at this particular moment, I was trying to build whatever bridge I could before he was lost again in the mosh pit of mudslingers, sycophants, and internet trolls. But it didn't make any difference. I don't know if he heard me. I think he could tell I was heading for the nearest exit ramp. Breathless, placating, he grasped at that last moment in the spotlight.

"We love you, Don Lemon! Black people love you!"

"I thank you so much for joining us."

"We love you, Don! We love CNN!"

"My heart goes out for you," I said.

In fact, my heart was breaking, for all of us, as the control room cut away to a commercial.

A few weeks later, I saw reports that Stevante had been arrested for threatening a neighbor, causing some property damage, and brandishing a long knife that people kept referring to as a "machete" even though it looked like a prop from an Errol Flynn movie. He livestreamed the knife bit on Facebook, standing by himself in a suburban side yard, his phone in selfie mode, a lonely dog barking somewhere down the quiet street. It was like seeing someone disappear into murky water.

Black Americans have an intimate relationship with death; they know loss and what it is to be left behind. A Black funeral is a beautiful thing to experience, because that marrow-deep understanding moans from the very bones of the mourners and reverberates in the rafters above the choir. The grief is unchained by WASPish inhibition. The music is soulful, older than pipe organs and church pews. White choirs try to co-opt songs like "Go Tell It on the Mountain" and "Swing Low, Sweet Chariot," but they never truly succeed.

In the late 1800s, White Protestant choirs began to sing a "negro spiritual" that, in their minds, spoke of the Rapture — that day at the End of Days, when a resolutely White Jesus would return to Earth, kicking butt and taking names.

My Lord, what a morning
When the stars begin to fall!

But the original version of this song goes back much further. The song as it is cited in *The Souls of Black Folk* by W. E. B. Du Bois is from an 1867 collection simply titled *Slave Songs of the United States*:

> *Oh, you will hear the trumpet sound*
> *To wake the nations underground.*
> *My Lord, what a mourning*
> *When the stars begin to fall!*

It was "mourning" they waited for, not "morning." The apparent scriptural source of the song (Amos 8:9–10) speaks of a time when corruption, cruelty, and greed have reached critical mass, and the feasts of the wicked turn to lamentations. You don't have to dig hard to get the subtext there. It was not about rapture; it was about reckoning.

The pandemic story picked up speed through the summer of 2020. While most of the world embraced the advice of scientists and quickly, effectively flattened the curve, people in the United States bickered in grocery stores over the wearing of masks and the efficacy of a bogus drug Trump kept pushing. With the death toll surpassing 160,000 souls, travelers from the US were barred from entering almost every other country in the world. Nonetheless, in an interview with Jonathan Swan of

Axios, Donald Trump insisted that everything was under control.

"How?" asked Swan, incredulous. "A thousand Americans are dying a day."

"They are dying. That's true. It is what it is," said Trump. "But that doesn't mean we aren't doing everything we can."

I was stunned by the sheer dearth of empathy in those words. *It is what it is.* This went beyond the self-defensive abjuration to which we all resort at times. When confronted with the reality of a thousand people dying every day, human nature raises an emotional firewall. We can't process it. Joseph Stalin famously said, "If one man dies of hunger, that is a tragedy. If millions die, that's only statistics."

In other words: "It is what it is."

I kept trying to put it in context: three plane crashes every day, the *Titanic* sinking four times a week, the entire population of Kansas City wiped out in a single summer. But that level of loss is so mind-boggling, we embrace a hazy dismay rather than face the pain.

"Gosh, that's so awful. Someone should do something about that."

We've seen this empathy desert over and over throughout the relatively brief history of the United States: the slave trade, the genocide of Indigenous peoples, gun violence, addiction to opiates, AIDS, and now COVID-19. The common denominator in all these situations is the tilted excess with which people of color are mortally impacted.

In 2020, Black people made up 13.4 percent of the total population of the United States, but 32 percent of people killed in lethal encounters with police—and 42 percent of the prisoners on death row—were Black.

The Black infant-mortality rate was double the rate of infant mortality among White, Asian, and Hispanic women, and Black children were 27 percent more likely to die in foster care.

Black women with breast cancer were 40 percent more likely to die than White women with breast cancer. In fact, according to the American Cancer Society: "African Americans have the highest death rate and shortest survival of any racial and ethnic group in the US for most cancers."

A few months into the pandemic, NPR reported: "Nationally, African American deaths from COVID-19 are nearly two times greater than would be expected based on their share of the population. In four states, the rate is three or more times greater."

And without even looking at the data—up goes the emotional firewall.

Our inability to process such gross injustice leaves us paralyzed, and our paralysis makes it easy for those in power to abdicate their responsibilities. So we get the pabulum of political rhetoric instead of meaningful root-and-stem solutions. The price we pay for the comfort of denial is the depersonalization of death and the death of empathy itself, particularly when it comes to the killing of Black people.

The loss of a sibling is a precise, localized agony, the loss of a reflected self. It goes to the bone in a way that people can easily relate to and empathize with. I'm not saying it's worse than any other loss, just different, in my experience. I lost my father when he was far too young to die. I witnessed my mother lose the love of her life and later saw her coping with the unimaginable loss of her child. I've learned that every loss wields unique impact—the inverse of that person's impact on your own life—and this, in microcosm, is the nexus of that urgent plea: *Black lives matter.* Because when Black lives truly do matter, in macrocosm, we won't have to hold up Black deaths to prove it.

The ways in which Black corpses have been displayed in this country is nothing short of pornography: the exhibition of something shockingly intimate for the purpose of eliciting a visceral physiological response. Innumerable examples parallel the development of technology over the centuries: During the slavery era, mutilated Black bodies were hoisted on pikes for the purpose of terrorizing other Black people into submission. During the years of Reconstruction following the Civil War, as a celebration of the Confederacy's unbroken spirit, Black bodies were tethered to horses or carriages and dragged down the same streets that were so thoughtfully muted with straw in deference to the death of a White resident. The Jim Crow era gave rise to a macabre industry of mass-produced lynching postcards featuring photographs of Black bodies hanging, burning, and dismembered—quaint souvenirs still prized by White supremacists today—purely for entertainment.

In the midst of the most recent social media renaissance, it's right to examine the true purpose and effect of distributing graphic images of Black people being murdered, like the final moments of Stephon Clark and George Floyd and the cell phone video of Ahmaud Arbery being gunned down by racist "vigilantes" while jogging in his own neighborhood. As a journalist, I'm focused on the imperative of conveying the true story of these incidents to the public. We need to know the objective truth of what happened, not the reflexively self-justifying version of events espoused by the officers involved and championed by knee-jerk law-and-order conservatives.

At the same time, it's our responsibility to provide context, lest those images convey the same chilling message as the bloody pikes posted downriver from Baton Rouge: *Know your place, Black child, or this could be you.*

Moreover, I question the true purpose and effect of

people watching those videos over and over and over again. At what point does desensitization kick in? At what point are we feeding the malevolent proclivities of those who consume with mouth-watering gratification what is, in essence, a snuff film? At what point do we stop staring at these grotesque, dehumanizing images and start taking a hard look at the society that sowed this bitter harvest?

The possession of and potential to distribute this type of footage presents a profound responsibility to both the media and the public. It is inarguable that graphic violence captured on film near the Edmund Pettus Bridge on Bloody Sunday opened the eyes of many White people to the truth of Black Americans' struggle for civil rights. And it's inarguable that the shocking footage of the murders of Ahmaud Arbery and George Floyd brought people to the streets in numbers unheard of and with fervor unseen before the summer of 2020.

What matters is where we go from here.

It is good that White people join the protests as White conscience continues to awaken, but please, tell me, my White brothers and sisters, at what point will your White conscience cease to require lurid images of Black suffering? Please, my Black brothers and sisters, tell me at what point our activism will cease to require holding up our own as martyrs?

Objectification is objectification; it doesn't matter if you're casting a person as saint or sinner. How can we stand in such awe of a person's death, yet show so little regard for the truth of their life?

When people impose a lot of "another angel in Heaven" religiosity on the dead, I understand that it's meant as balm for sorrow, but I allow myself no such daydreams. Among the questions that still plague my soul regarding my sister's death, there is one true thing I know for sure: she went down fighting. My sister is not some ethereal, harp-strumming angel; she is a lioness who lives on in her children and grandchildren, who served her country with her boots on the ground, served her community with her heart wide open, and helped her little brother with his homework. I will not rob her of her fierceness in an attempt to sideslip the undertow of my own sorrow.

That's why I can't forget that small moment when Shai'Ellesse Works tried so hard to tell us about who her brother really was: an amazing child who was smart beyond smart but still needed his big sister's help sometimes. Here is where I feel the keenest loss, the dissipation of a thousand dreams, the squandering of unlimited potential. This is where I see the jagged rending of a great tapestry that includes the threads of my life and my sister's, just as surely as it includes your life and the lives of George, Ahmaud, Stephon, and Stevante.

The next tragic headline isn't happening on television. It's happening all around us at this very moment.

Black. *Lives*. Matter.

Real lives. Not postcard ghosts or graffiti angels. Real people, who deserve equal opportunities to breathe and be heard, to work and prosper, to learn from mistakes, contribute to the greater good, and thrive in an atmosphere of security, peace, and dignity.

According to the Kübler-Ross model, denial is the first stage of grief, followed by anger, bargaining, depression, and acceptance. If we lack the fortitude, individually and as a society, to move past that first stage, the compulsory process of grieving will be truncated and internalized, and we will remain suspended in a state of dangerous self-delusion and disconsolate loss.

So that's where we go from here: we find it within ourselves to process this fundamental reckoning, lay the dead to rest, and turn our tearstained faces toward the good and necessary challenges of living.

4

Seeking Justice in the Land of Law and Order

When White supremacist Dylann Roof was arrested after gunning down nine people at Emanuel African Methodist Episcopal Church in Charleston, South Carolina, in 2015, he was steered into the police cruiser with a protective hand on his head. When Eric Garner, a 44-year-old Black man, was arrested for selling individual cigarettes from a pack without a tax stamp, he was thrown to the ground in an illegal choke hold, gasping an all-too-familiar refrain—*"I can't breathe!"*—until he died facedown on the sidewalk.

When I spoke with Garner's mother, Gwen Carr, at the height of the George Floyd demonstrations, she said,

"It's like an echo from the grave. George Floyd saying the same words my son said. My son begged for his life. George Floyd begged for his life. He even called out for his mother...so I say to that—that he was calling out for all of us mothers, that we should take a stand."

Demonstrations continued to ebb and flow through the long, hot summer of 2020. Every night, I tried to bring moments of levity and introspection to my show, knowing that viewers were being whipsawed by conflicting images of fire and song, hope and cynicism, peaceful protest and the kind of smash-and-grab looting that happens when latent hopelessness meets golden opportunity. The majority of protesters were peaceful and united, focused on police brutality as the core issue, which is entirely reasonable. Adjusting for population, Black people are killed during encounters far more often than White people are killed, and this says nothing of the rate at which Black people are harassed, pulled over, shaken down, humiliated, and mistreated during processing.

"Defund the police!" became the battle cry, and frankly, it made me cringe. Look, I get it. I'm all about reinventing the way police are present in the lives and neighborhoods of Black people, but in my opinion, "defund the police" is not a productive thing to say. It promotes a startled knee-jerk response, potentially alienating people who might have been allies, and it implies an unrealistic snap-of-the-fingers simplicity for those who are willing to fight for change but can't stomach the long haul. You don't gain a hundred pounds eating one bag of M&M's, and you're not gonna lose a hundred pounds with one hour on your Peloton. It's a process, whichever direction you're headed.

I knew the moment I heard this catchphrase that Trump and his enablers would seize on and exploit it. With the branding proficiency of snake-oil salesmen, they immediately released a campaign ad featuring an apocryphal 911 call answered by an officious voicemail message: "Due to defunding of the police department, we're sorry, but no one is here to take your call. If you're calling to report a *rape*, please press 1..."

This was gratuitous drivel, of course, ignoring the fact that 911 and "the police" are not the same thing. No one ever suggested defunding 911 services, which dispatches different resources—fire, ambulance, animal control, etc.— for different problems. Diverting tax dollars toward targeted solutions rather than a one-Glock-fits-all police presence actually makes a great deal of *conservative* common sense. Taxpayers would spend less and reap greater benefits if problems were addressed by teams trained and equipped to handle specific problem areas.

If your house is on fire, you are best served by trained firefighters with specialized equipment and practical knowledge pertaining to fire suppression. We've already figured that out. Take the next logical steps: If the imaginary caller in the bogus campaign ad presses 1, she would be best served by a trained sexual assault team. A domestic disturbance would be best addressed by trained domestic abuse teams. And police officers themselves would be better off if they were not being asked to solve every situation from fender bender to bank robbery.

I believe the majority of police officers are well-intentioned individuals who go into this job with benevolent—or at least, benign—objectives. I'm certain very, very few men and women pursue a career in law enforcement with the goal of making their community less safe and more chaotic. But, clearly, many of them become overwhelmed and jaded, taken in by a violent culture that combines a dark history with a series of impossible missions. Their superiors send them out to deal with situations for which they have neither adequate training nor appropriate tools and, in doing so, rob them of the opportunity to live up to the ideals that drew them (theoretically) toward this vocation.

The most readily available coping mechanism is the dehumanization of the people they are sworn to protect, but the cost of dehumanizing others is a chunk of your own humanity. It would appear that too many police officers have bartered their conscience, pressured by a "thin blue line" of peers, perhaps telling themselves that they had to cede some portion of their soul in order to survive.

Avocation is what you do. Vocation is who you are. We feed police officers into a system where the two get twisted in dangerous and demoralizing ways. The ideology with which we currently deploy police in major cities is tantamount to excising a melanoma with a blowtorch. In neighborhoods where racial bias shapes police response, Black people are still being admonished to "go slow" as they push for change. But how much more slowly could we have gone? And what has been the reward for the virtue of patience?

From the beginning, police work as we know it was not about maintaining public safety; it was about maintaining social order. "Professionalized organizations"—slave patrols and self-proclaimed guardians of the antebellum lifestyle—made their presence felt as far back as 1690, when laws authorized any White person to detain any Black person suspected of being a runaway slave.

Chenjerai Kumanyika is an assistant professor in Rutgers University's Department of Journalism and Media Studies and host of the podcast *Uncivil*, which reexamines the history of the Civil War. Chenjerai told me that pre–Civil War slave patrols were baked into the origins of modern policing, beginning with the formation of the Boston Police Department in 1838. In 1854, the Philadelphia Police Department was founded with strict advertised rules: *No immigrants.*

"And you know, no Black people were on that force, right?" said Chenjerai. We laughed together at the very notion. "Those police departments were created to keep those people in line, not to protect them. Even when those people were facing violence, facing Jim Crow, facing lynching, facing poverty—if they got out of line, they would be brought back into line by the police."

According to Chenjerai, it's historically accurate to say that policing was created to protect and serve the majority of White middle- and working-class people, but for Black folks, policing meant the opposite of public safety. In the 1890s, a Senate committee investigation uncovered rampant corruption in politics and law enforcement. (Think *Gangs of New York*.) In response, August Vollmer, a veteran of the Spanish-American War and the first police chief in Berkeley, California, led a law-enforcement renaissance. Remembered as the "father of modern policing," Vollmer pushed for sweeping reforms, evolved a military-style command structure, and implemented scientific methodology and state-of-the-art investigative techniques. He established a strong moral code, wanting police officers to be seen as noble and benevolent, respected but not feared.

"He brought order and professionalism and dignity," Chenjerai said, "but in service of what? In service to *whom?*"

If you're living in a Jim Crow society and the police bring order to that, all you have is a nice, orderly Jim Crow society. A repudiation of that same old, same old has been stomping American streets for fifty years.

* * * *

In late August 2020, another White police officer shot another Black man in Kenosha, Wisconsin, and another viral video inflamed a nation already at the jagged edge of exhaustion.

The video shows 29-year-old Jacob Blake on the ground, surrounded by officers. Blake manages to get up from what we later learned was a hard jolt from a taser. He strides away from the officers, rounds the front of the vehicle, and opens the driver's door of his car, with his three small children inside. Officer Rusten Sheskey, who later said he thought there might be a knife in the car, seizes the back of Blake's tee shirt and fires seven bullets point-blank into Blake's torso. Blake survived but was left paralyzed from the waist down. An added twist of irony upon insult upon injury: police shackled Blake's useless legs to his hospital bed.

The following day, with freshly fueled protests raging across the country, Blake's sister, Letetra Widman, stood before the press, dry-eyed and resolute.

"So many people have reached out to me, telling me they're sorry this happened to my family," she said. "Well, don't be sorry, 'cause this has been happening to my family for a long time. Longer than I can account for. It happened to Emmett Till. Emmett Till is my family. Philando. Mike Brown. Sandra. This has been happening to my family, and I have shed tears for every single one of these people that this has happened to. This is nothing new. I'm not sad. I'm not sorry. I'm *angry*. And I'm tired. I haven't cried one time. I stopped crying years ago. I am numb. I have been watching police murder people who look like me for years. I'm also a Black History minor, so not only have I been watching it for the thirty years that I've been on this planet, but I've been watching it for years before we were even alive. I'm not sad. I don't want your pity. I want change."

Civic unrest ramped up again. There were peaceful protests by day, but at night, looters and shit-disturbers took to the streets. The National Guard was activated, curfews were implemented, and we began to see the disturbing presence of self-proclaimed "militia" groups: swaggering cadres of White men with pistols on their hips and semi-automatic long guns dangling from their shoulders. Social media bristled with photos and videos of state and federal officers interacting with these armed men, greeting them and giving them water bottles.

One officer was videotaped saying to a group of White men, "We appreciate you guys. We really do." He tosses water bottles to them as another officer scolds protesters to get off the street. Fifteen minutes later, one of the young White men, Kyle Rittenhouse—a baby-faced 17-year-old armed with a military-style semi-automatic rifle—shot and killed two unarmed White protesters. As he walked away from their bodies, several protesters screamed repeatedly at passing police vehicles, "That guy just killed someone!" Rittenhouse raised his hands in the air, like Rocky on the steps of the Philadelphia Museum of Art, and proceeded calmly down the street as police vehicles cruised by without pumping a brake.

Rittenhouse was eventually arrested at his home without incident and charged with first-degree murder. Within forty days, the Christian crowdfunding site GiveSendGo had collected more than $535,000 on just one of several pages raising money for his defense. Jacob Blake's mother put up a page on GoFundMe for her son's legal and medical expenses. It raised over two million dollars in its first forty days. The blatant disparity in the way these two young men were treated by police shines an unforgiving light on the system, but these levels of financial support would seem to suggest that the tide of public opinion may be evolving.

"It feels different now," Gwen Carr said.

She told me she experienced a surge of hope when she saw the diversity of the protesters and the myriad ways in which people were expressing their anger, hope, and resolve.

"To demonstrate is beautiful," she said, "but after demonstration should come legislation. That's where we will get the changes."

Breonna Taylor was a "soft target," according to investigators; the 26-year-old paramedic with no dogs or children was expected to be home alone, posing minimal risk. For reasons that will never be clear, a no-knock warrant was issued to Louisville Metro Police as part of a narcotics investigation involving Breonna's ex-boyfriend. They knew the ex wasn't there; he was being arrested across town at the same time plainclothes officers approached Breonna's apartment with a battering ram.

At first, LMPD claimed the officers weren't wearing body cameras. Later, when photographs showed that, in fact, some body cameras were worn, LMPD claimed that the cameras weren't active. Lacking that footage—for whatever reason—we're left with skeletal facts supported by physical and ballistic evidence: At 12:40 am, Breonna was asleep in bed with her current boyfriend, Kenneth Walker, a postal worker. Jolted from sleep, they assumed an intruder was breaking in and did what you would do: they called 911. It didn't even occur to them that the assailants crashing through the door were cops. Kenneth fired one "warning shot" from his legally carried weapon, aiming low and striking one of the officers in the leg. Officers answered with a hail of gunfire. When it was over, Breonna lay dead on the floor in her hallway, her body riddled with bullets. Coroners placed her time of death at 12:48 am, but evidence indicates that she was left there, bleeding, for up to twenty minutes before she died.

For a long time, it seemed to Breonna's mother, Tamika Palmer, that nobody cared. Tamika's lawyer, civil rights attorney Ben Crump, made a valiant attempt to get it into the media, but it wasn't until months later that the story finally got some real traction. On the rising tide of national outcry in response to the murders of George Floyd and Ahmaud Arbery, people began to chant Breonna's name. We saw her face on social media, murals, and the cover of O, *The Oprah Magazine*.

In the long history of American police violence, we've seen the deconstruction wizards uphold a sturdy tradition of spinning blame in the direction of the victim. But how, we wondered, could anyone argue the foundationless killing of a first responder who was *sleeping in her bed* when she was attacked? How could anyone deny the shoddy police work that led to such a catastrophic blunder? Month after month, Tamika Palmer waited for justice. We all waited, but we waited with the jaded heaviness of those who've waited too long too many times.

Emmett Till was murdered by a lynch mob on August 28, 1955. About three weeks later, on September 23, an all-male, all-White jury acquitted the killers after deliberating for sixty-seven minutes.

"If we hadn't stopped to drink pop," one juror drawled, "it wouldn't have taken that long."

Breonna Taylor was murdered on March 13, 2020. On September 23—after more than six months in which seventy-five days of nonstop demonstrations resulted in the arrest and filing of charges against more than five hundred protesters—sixty-five years to the day after the acquittal of the men who killed Emmett Till, a grand jury declined to move forward with charges against the police officers directly involved in Breonna Taylor's death. They did, however, indict an officer for firing bullets that damaged drywall in the apartment of Breonna's White neighbors.

Coming just a few days after the death of Ruth Bader Ginsburg and overshadowed by immediate moves to cram a conservative justice onto the Supreme Court to replace her, the Breonna Taylor decision felt like the death of justice itself. In a statement read to the press by Breonna's aunt, Tamika Palmer said she never had faith in the system.

"When I speak on it, I'm considered an angry Black woman," she said. "But know this: I am angry."

She went on to list all the ways in which the system had failed Breonna, from the dubious warrant to the way Breonna was left to lie, almost naked, bleeding out on the floor, while officers fumbled through her things rather than render assistance that she, as a paramedic, would have rendered to any one of them.

"I hope you never know the pain of knowing your child is in need of help, and you're not able to get help," said Tamika. "I hope you never know the pain of your child being murdered 191 days in a row."

That night, I spoke with Ben Crump as he stood inside

the jetway, preparing to board a flight so he could be with Tamika and her family.

"Ben, I know you're traveling now," I said. "I appreciate your doing this on the platform. If you could raise your camera a little bit, because—thank you, sir."

It's telling, I think, that I had to ask him to frame his face as you would for a selfie; most people would have centered themselves, focused on how they would look on TV. Ben keeps his eye literally and figuratively on the prize. We parsed the details of Breonna's case—the tragedy of her death and the travesty of the legal outcome—and then he offered a blunt summation.

"You have the piss-poor three Ps in this situation," said Ben. "You have the policy, you have the policing, and you have the prosecution."

This is the big picture too many people are missing when they focus, pro or con, on defunding, abolishing, or reforming the police. Yes, police brutality is a problem, and it makes for lurid clickbait and dramatic TV. But you want to see some real violence being done? Check out a monotone C-SPAN video of members of Congress passing a bill that panders to provincial voters while dumping guns into the inner cities, and then flip to a conservative news outlet for the running narrative about Black on Black crime. Invest an hour in a long read about how the CIA purposely funneled inexpensive powdered cocaine into the Black neighborhoods of Los Angeles in the 1980s.

Open a spreadsheet that shows the outrageously skewed manner in which Black men, women, and children are incarcerated for petty crimes and marijuana use that wouldn't leave a wrinkle on a White guy's résumé.

Statistics aren't sexy. They don't fall under the old journalism trope: "If it bleeds, it leads." But we will never solve this problem if we maintain our myopic focus on individual incidents of police brutality. Police reforms dating all the way back to the days of August Vollmer have done exactly zero to rectify the swirling Charybdis in which policy, policing, and prosecution form an inescapable vortex that sucks Black communities into a system from which they cannot hope to emerge whole.

This time, our objective has to be bigger than curbing police conduct. This time, it has to be about creating a culture of *justice*.

Ras Baraka grew up in a Newark neighborhood where he witnessed numerous bloody encounters between police and Black activists, including his parents. Today he's the mayor of Newark, which puts him in charge of policy, police, and prosecutors. I walk a similar line between journalism and activism. I have to put the story out there and ask a question. Sometimes people get mad, and everyone has an opinion about how I should have handled it differently or done more on the side of right. Like Ras Baraka, I have activism in my blood. So I get the dilemma he's in.

"I don't have the luxury of pessimism," Ras told me. "I have to fix it."

"As a Black mayor," I said, "do you see the problem more clearly than perhaps a White mayor?"

"Yes," he said. "I was born and raised in Newark. I had problems with the police myself as a young man growing up in a city, being stopped, searched, even abused, beaten. So when people say that this is happening, it's not like a surprise to me. I'm not like, *Oh, is this really going on?* I know that it's real and that we need to address it."

Since Ras Baraka became mayor in 2014, body cameras, a civilian review board, and other reforms have reduced complaints against the police by 80 percent, which has saved taxpayers millions of dollars.

This is where someone like Ben Crump comes into play, representing the families of Breonna Taylor, Ahmaud Arbery, Trayvon Martin, George Floyd, Jacob Blake, and others failed by a legal system in which the "mills of the Lord's justice" don't grind evenly for Black and White plaintiffs. When policy, policing, and prosecution fail, he brings the only hammer he has left: punitive damages. He wages war in a three-piece suit, filing civil suits for wrongful death and injury damages justifiably in the millions, hoping that sooner or later, White taxpayers will see the pragmatic value

of standing with their neighbors of color to demand meaningful systemic change. Breonna Taylor's family was eventually awarded $12 million, which is certainly not adequate
compensation for the loss of someone you love, but perhaps
enough to open someone else's eyes.

The concept of defunding the police is the flip side of
the same coin, a preemptive approach to the same problem.
If it works.

When I asked Ras Baraka if he thought defunding the
police was a viable way forward, he nodded, thoughtful.

"It's wise to begin thinking about alternative forms of
policing," he said. "Democratically, we have to fight for
the police to actually do their job, number one, and
number two, not kill us in the process. We need police.
But we need them to be different."

Different how? is the question. That campaign ad with
the bogus 911 call got a lot of traction, because it scissored
into the natural grain of human nature, slicing a neat line
between fear of harm and need for normalcy. A lot of
Black folks are not comfortable with the police presence
in their neighborhoods, but they have an even deeper fear
of what would happen if the police weren't there. That's
what they know. Anything else feels unfamiliar. We
haven't had the opportunity to see what might happen if
we didn't have White influencers micromanaging things in
a way that's not helpful.

A lot of effort, media, and money have been invested

in the characterization of Black neighborhoods as danger-ous, crime-riddled, the "bad part of town" where you can't walk your dog after dusk. I don't hear anyone putting forth the seemingly naïve theorem: If a neighborhood gets worse as policies increase police presence and unfairly tilt prosecution, doesn't it stand to reason that the neighbor-hood would improve if policy decreased police presence and fairly redressed prosecution?

"We have to convince them that it's plausible," said Ras, "and that we have the ideas and the resources to actually make that happen."

Thinking about the police officers and officials I'd spoken with in the weeks since George Floyd's murder, I said, "Police are sensitive right now—some would say rightfully so—because they feel like they're being targeted, getting hurt, maybe even killed because people don't respect the police anymore. Is that a fair assessment in your opinion?"

"I think it's ridiculous," Ras said without diffidence. "First, I want to say: *Join the club.* I mean, we've been targeted for hundreds of years. You know? We've been *uncomfortable.* We've been profiled. The evidence shows that. It is clear. And I think they need to really listen to what's happening. Police agencies—not just officers, the *agencies,* the people in charge—need to really pay attention. Sit down, take heed, and begin to make some real constructive and transformative changes in their

THIS IS THE FIRE

departments. Suck up everything—the feelings, the resentment, the ego, all that thing—and deal with what's going on that is a direct result of their behavior."

I suspect the response to that would be something on the order of: "I won't do it anymore. Policing is not the same, and I don't want to lose my life over it." But when I pointed this out to Ras, he said he believed this transformation would ultimately improve the lives of police officers.

"I think a civilian review board makes police safer," he said. "I think body cameras make police safer."

I sat back and thought about the immediacy with which those pragmatic measures might change the way police engage with a community. It makes plain sense that a society moving in the right direction will need less police intervention. Partnering with community members to recognize over-policing where and when it happens, solving issues of inequality, inequity, and insecurity, figuring out alternative responses to social problems— suddenly it does seem possible for a neighborhood to get off the carousel of violence, distrust, and conflict.

The city of Newark recently committed 5 percent of its police budget to create an Office of Violence Prevention, where social workers, mental health professionals, and other trained personnel will respond to situations before they escalate. I see changes like this happening across the country as protests push for progress that was probably inevitable but far too slow in coming. Calls for "law and order," along with the mobilization of troops into cities to quell demonstrations, failed to recognize the difference between "order" and "subjugation."

What does "law and order" look like? People cowering from iron-fisted abuse and a dysfunctional system? No. *Law* happens when duly elected officials create civil and penal codes that apply to all people equally. *Order* happens when we all abide by a social contract that respects all people equally.

This doesn't happen in one heated moment of political upheaval. We have to be in this for the long haul. It starts with a willingness to reimagine our system of justice; at some point, we have to start talking about what *should* exist instead of rehashing what should not. We need to get loud and accept that some folks don't like our loudness, but our impassioned mobilization must be followed by long-term engagement in the political process—demonstration leading to legislation, as Gwen Carr envisioned.

"Real change, enduring change, happens one step at a time," said the Notorious RBG.

This is work. Real work. Mule work. But listen—it's not like we've never had to reinvent ourselves before. Reinvention, for better or worse, is the essence of American experience, and it is that to the tenth power for Black Americans. The choice before us now is a new era of parity and peace or a cynical recycling of the old "go slow."

5

Of Movies, Myths, and Monuments

General Williams Carter Wickham was a reluctant rebel; he voted against secession in 1861. When his fellow delegates approved Virginia's resolution to leave the United States, however, Wickham stepped up to command a Confederate cavalry division and was elected to the Second Confederate Congress. Wickham's letters (archived in the Special Collections at Virginia Tech) show that immediately after the official end of the Civil War, he renounced the Confederate cause and vowed allegiance to the Republicans. He became the president of a burgeoning railroad empire, expanded his agricultural dealings, and served as a United States senator until his death in 1888.

Wickham was born and died at Hickory Hill, a 3,300-acre plantation, where he raised the next generation of his affluent Southern family with his wife, Lucy. Like my own forefather, Wickham also had a host of descendants who never made it into the family Bible. He fathered six children by a slave woman called Bibanna.

In 1891, three years after his death, a statue of Wickham was installed in Monroe Park in Richmond, Virginia. The *Norfolk Landmark* covered the unveiling and described the seventeen-foot monument as "suggestive in every particular of that solidity, massiveness, and determination that characterized General Wickham." It was an "artistic triumph," they said. "Very impressive and realistic." The eight-foot square pedestal was inscribed:

WICKHAM
"Soldier, Statesman, Patriot, Friend"

Wickham's sword was stolen in 1956. Other than that, he stood forever battle-ready in full Confederate bombast with a pair of field glasses in one hand, poised for reconnoiter, and a pair of gloves in the other, as if he was prepared to hurl the proverbial gauntlet.

I recently spoke with two of Wickham's descendants: 67-year-old musician/storyteller Reggie Harris, a Black descendant of Wickham and Bibanna, and 28-year-old Clayton Wickham, the White great-great-great-grandson of Wickham and Lucy. Reggie says the ongoing dialogue about their shared family history and how it reflects the broader history of the United States has been a "powerful, heart-shifting experience." He sings about it in "Hickory Hill," a song he wrote after visiting the old plantation with several of his White Wickham relatives:

So now our stories come together
Across these fields of broken dreams...

"We can't change history," Reggie told me. "We can't alter what is true. We, in fact, are related. What we decided, on that day and every time we talk, is that we won't let that history define us. But we have to acknowledge it."

Clayton Wickham says there was "a lot of silence" about the Confederacy when he was growing up.

"For much of my childhood, I didn't even really know he was there in that park," he said. "I can remember my middle school teacher telling us explicitly during our history class that the Civil War was not about slavery."

"Yeah, it's not about slavery." I had to laugh. I grew up hearing the same party line applied to the Confederate flags and Robert E. Lee High School in Baton Rouge. "It's about Southern pride, right? Is that the story?"

"Southern pride," he nodded. "States' rights. It's framed as a kind of patriotism, and people ignore the fact that the patriotism was grounded in White supremacy. But I also think that there are people like me and my family members whose complicity in White supremacy is partly due to ignorance. And to some extent that ignorance is willful. Because I think, as a White person, there have been times in my life where I've just turned my head."

The moment when Clayton could no longer look away came in August 2017, when self-identified neo-Nazis, White nationalists, and others who shared alt-right ideology descended on Charlottesville, Virginia, for the Unite the Right rally only a few weeks after a resurgent Ku Klux Klan marched there with Confederate flags and white robes. Faith-based organizations and civil rights activists came from far and wide to stand with local merchants, students, and University of Virginia faculty in peaceful counterprotests. After state police ordered the crowd to disperse, 20-year-old James Alex Fields Jr. intentionally plowed his 2010 Dodge Challenger into a group of counterprotesters, injuring nineteen people and killing 32-year-old Heather Heyer.

The final post on Heather's Facebook profile said: "If you're not outraged, you're not paying attention." And finally, Clayton Wickham was.

Within days, Clayton and his younger brother Will, who grew up on Monument Avenue in Richmond, emailed Mayor Levar Stoney and all nine members of the city council, stating their position as Wickham's living legacy: "The removal of these statues is long overdue."

The brothers were not alone. The Reverend Robert W. Lee IV and other descendants of Confederate stalwarts have also spoken out, requesting the removal of monuments and decrying the slow-to-nonexistent response from local officials, who drag their feet for fear of alienating conservative voters. Three years after Clayton and Will petitioned for the removal of the Wickham monument, the general was still standing, impassive as ever, on his pedestal—until the summer of 2020, when protesters slung ropes around the thick, cast-bronze neck and heaved the statue off its perch. Wickham lay sprawled on his back, half on the manicured lawn, half on the grit pathway. Tattooed with white and orange spray paint, his resolute expression was transformed to an air of startled dismay.

This was the first of several Confederate monuments torn down in Richmond, where peaceful protesters had spent the day speaking, listening, singing, and cooking out in the shade cast by the massive statue of Robert E. Lee on horseback that towers above Monument Avenue. At the time, Virginia hosted more Confederate monuments than any other state in the union, a dubious distinction that protesters were determined to change. Weary of waiting for state and local governments to do the right thing, protesters across the country were taking matters into their own hands.

"We have an opportunity to take another step forward," said Reggie. "Maybe, now that the statues have come down, the conversation is reopened. Maybe we can use this opportunity to make a new start."

On the Fourth of July, Donald Trump stood in front of Mount Rushmore, bawling out those who'd engaged in this "merciless campaign to defame our heroes, erase our values, and indoctrinate our children."

I'm willing to own that. If your heroes are murderers and armed insurrectionists who sought to overthrow the United States government by force and violence, I hereby volunteer for a merciless campaign to defame them. If your values are grounded in White supremacy, yes, let's erase that. If your children never heard about the German Coast Uprising or Sojourner Truth, if they were taught in school that this country was torn in two—and is now being torn in two again—over some nebulous tenet of "states' rights" and that neo-Nazis from Michigan display Confederate flags for the sake of "Southern Pride," then I pray for their indoctrination.

The mythology of White supremacy rode into the South on bronze horses during Reconstruction, but let's not pretend folks up North ignored the hoofbeats.

In *The Devil Finds Work*, James Baldwin wrote: "I cannot be blamed for an ignorance which an entire republic had deliberately inculcated." Mythology is the modus of that inculcation, satisfying our need for stories that sedate the conscience, setting up patterns whereby we deconstruct and justify circumstances as needed. The myth of julep-fueled antebellum politesse, for example, promotes the laughable idea that slaves were happy, banjo-picking participants in some benevolent patriarchy. As the pattern evolves, the myth of good cops and bad neighborhoods sets the stage for a no-knock warrant leading to a terribly unfortunate misunderstanding for which no police officer could be held accountable.

More than 150 years after the official end of the Civil War, the United States is engaged in what many people call the uncivil war, an unceasing pitched battle over the same old issue: White supremacy. Now, as then, the trenches are dug by goaded fears, learned hatred, loaded rhetoric, and bare-knuckled politics. The foot soldiers — desperately angry on one side, desperately ignorant on the other — are the distant children of obsolete martyrs and forgotten foes. It's no longer a war between North and South, and it never was a war between Black and White; it is an ideological conflict between those who cling to a barbaric ethnic caste system and those who are determined to progress beyond it.

Greed has always been and will always be the soul of this struggle. Its architects are oligarchs who raise up generals without decency and lieutenants for whom decency is a minor inconvenience. As in every war, the first and last blood spilled is the thinnest: slum scions without pedigree, poets without a dime, scholars clinging to their threadbare standards, and a *World War Z* horde of marching bereaved and walking wounded. Those on the front lines have no motivation but the stories they've been told: myths and legends presented in middle school textbooks that should be subtitled "A Redacted History of the United States" or maybe "A Conveniently Selective Memory of What Went Down."

Faced with the challenge of reuniting South Africa after apartheid, Nelson Mandela created the Truth and Reconciliation Commission (TRC) as part of the Promotion of National Unity and Reconciliation Act in 1995. Under this umbrella, a Human Rights Committee conducted nationally televised hearings allowing those who'd suffered human rights abuses to be heard, ensuring that recorded history would reflect what actually happened to Black people under apartheid. An Amnesty Committee considered petitions for pardon so that some of those—not all—who'd committed human rights abuses could be forgiven, ensuring that White people would be able to embrace a post-apartheid society without fear. A Reparation and Rehabilitation Committee worked on finding ways to restore dignity and, in some cases, property. Knowing that justice in its narrowest "eye for an eye" definition was not possible, Mandela focused on cultivating Black forgiveness and White empathy as a way forward. Results achieved by the TRC are still being debated, but it was an indisputably powerful first step away from civil war and stands as a revolutionary act of covenant and absolution.

Empathy is key to the kind of social evolution we can and should strive for in this moment, and if we're going to change the American capacity for empathy, we must question storytelling that adheres to the old caste system of heroes and villains. We must challenge iconography based on tropes of conscious and subconscious White supremacy. These tropes are inherited, embedded in family lore and religious mythology, written so deep in our bones we don't even flinch when we see them play out. So those tropes need to be called out. It doesn't matter if the storyteller's intention was malevolent or benign, blatant or subtle. If those tropes are woven into it, the effect is the same: perpetuation of ideas that undermine the struggle for justice and equality.

"Correlation does not imply causation," as they say in the study of statistics, but correlation does imply co-relation. Without implying cause and effect, it's worth our time to examine how images and ideas coexist in the same cultural ecosystem.

THIS IS THE FIRE

* * * *

I'm a huge film nerd. I grew up watching classic black-and-white movies and TV shows with my mom. Even though I almost never saw characters who looked like me in these old films, I always found elements of character that resonated for me. I could relate to the curiosity of Charlie Chan, the derring-do of Captain Blood, and the stalwart uprightness of Mingo, all of whom were played by White actors.

My mom prefers old movies over new ones, which are "full of all the killings and shootings and cursing." She'd rather see the gauzy noir malfeasance in *The Maltese Falcon* or *Casablanca*. I get that, too. There is something of an oasis in those grayscale images and tinny soundtracks. Sometimes, at the end of a long day, I'll send Mom a text: "Hey! *Double Indemnity* is on TV."

She's willing to turn it on, no matter how late the hour.

"I'm a nighthawk," she says.

We get on the phone and watch it together, chatting back and forth. If Mom sees a Black person on the screen, she texts me immediately: "Gee whiz! They got one in there."

Of course, the Black person is almost always in the background, quickly passed over, and their lines have little substance beyond the service they're rendering to the White movie star.

"Or they're dancing," Mom says wryly.

She's saddened by the fact that great Black actors never had the opportunity to play roles that would have presented strong Black characters.

"They were not being portrayed as an image for Black children," Mom says. "That they can make it in life and be other than a maid or a cook, or whatever they are."

People always told Mom she looked like Lena Horne, and Mom loved that, but she always wondered what Lena Horne could have achieved—how the lives of both these beautiful women could have been different—if Mom, as a teenager, could have seen Lena Horne performing the kind of roles that propelled lesser talents to stardom.

Lena Horne proved herself in her nightclub acts and a series of small films with all-Black casts, but the roles she played in her seven major films with MGM were carefully contained in nonessential scenes that were removed for segregated Southern theaters. Hear me now: they actually invested the time and budget required to remove her beautifully crafted scenes! It simply wouldn't do to have a glamorous Black starlet towering over an audience full of White faces; that might have given a Black girl in the balcony uppity ideas.

During WWII, Ms. Horne was kicked off a USO tour when she complained about Black American soldiers being seated behind German prisoners of war. She continued touring anyway, paying for it herself. When the war was over, she worked with Eleanor Roosevelt on anti-lynching legislation. In 1963, she stood with Martin Luther King and John Lewis at the March on Washington. If ever there was a great, golden goddess of a role model, it was Lena Horne. But Lena Horne was not the role model who fit the White supremacist narrative, so we got Aunt Jemima and Uncle Remus instead.

Mom refers to *Song of the South* as "that zip-a-dee-doo-dah mess." All these years later, it still gets under her skin.

"He's got all these little kids around," she says, "and he's reminiscing like slavery was so great, and I'm like, *really?*"

We watched these types of portrayals over and over again, because that's all there was. The alternative was to stay home and read books in which Black people were portrayed with dignity and respect, like *Huckleberry*—oh. No. Bad example.

Okay, like *To Kill a Mocking*—whoa. Even worse.

Catcher in the...no. That's a WASP's nest.

Moby...okay, forget it.

When I was a kid, the few Black characters I read about in books or saw on television and in the movies were nothing like the Black people I saw in my real-life Black community. Our neighbors were doctors, engineers, and business owners. My father was an attorney. The Black people I knew were well-educated, middle-class citizens. I never saw a Black neighborhood like mine on television, but I immediately recognized the White version of my world on *Leave It to Beaver.*

"What I didn't like is why we always had to be *Uncle* and *Mammy* in movies," says Mom. "Uncle who? Who's Mammy? I ain't none of your mammy. That bothered me. It was like we were always played down in everything."

As much as she disliked the Mammy stereotype, my mom still loved *Gone with the Wind* and bristled when it was temporarily removed from HBO Max in June 2020. She felt it was unfair to the Black actors, Hattie McDaniel, the first Black person to win an Oscar, and Butterfly ("I don't know nothin' 'bout birthin' no babies") McQueen, who, in Mom's estimation, stole the whole show. My take on McQueen's performance is closer to that of Malcolm X, who said, "When Butterfly McQueen went into her act, I felt like crawling under the rug."

Even more cringe-worthy were the performances of White actors in blackface, a grotesque practice that began in minstrel shows of old and somehow continued into the twenty-first century. I'll cut Judy Garland some slack for that "Way Down South" moment from *Everybody Sing* in 1938; she was only sixteen years old. But what's the excuse for Fred Armisen playing Barack Obama or Jimmy Fallon playing Chris Rock on *SNL*? Or Jimmy Kimmel playing Karl Malone and Oprah Winfrey on *The Man Show*? Remember the 2012 Oscars skit where Justin Bieber is hanging out with Sammy Davis Jr., played by Billy Crystal?

Recently several stars, including Jimmy Fallon, Sarah Silverman, and Jimmy Kimmel, have apologized for appearing in blackface, and that's a start. These onscreen portrayals shape expectations, reinforce stereotypes, and validate racist tropes that translate to real-life prejudices in the workplace, on the playground, and in encounters with law enforcement and the court system. But those portrayals are out there, from *Huckleberry Finn* to *Saturday Night Live,* and trying to erase them is not the answer.

For one thing, the moment we skew toward censorship or "cancel culture," we lose something of our most precious liberty: freedom of speech. I'm not about that. Moreover, if we erase those images—remove *Huck Finn* from school libraries, yank *Gone with the Wind* from streaming services—we create gaps in the essential story of how an economic system based on White supremacy developed in the United States and maintained its choke hold on us well into modern times. The damage has been done. We can't undo it. We can learn from it only if we face it for what it was.

Context is key.

Gone with the Wind returned to HBO Max with a new introduction by film scholar Jacqueline Najuma Stewart, a professor of cinema studies at the University of Chicago, a host on Turner Classic Movies, and author of *Migrating to the Movies: Cinema and Black Urban Modernity,* which explores the evolution of Black characters, audience members, and behind-the-camera creators of film in the twentieth century. When I asked her to help me sort out my own love/hate relationship with Scarlett and Rhett, she didn't try to take anything away from the film itself.

"If you look at *Gone with the Wind,*" she said, "the costuming, set design—no expense was spared to produce this romantic image of the antebellum South. And then you have extraordinary acting in this film. It has this enduring quality as a classic. But I think what some of us have known all along, and more people are learning, is that we have to always look at these things through a historical lens."

Gone with the Wind operates as a historical document, not because of the bullshit portrayal of slavery and the nobility of the Confederate cause, but as an artifact of Depression-era Hollywood.

First, it stands as evidence of the highest level to which any actor of color could aspire in that moment: the Oscar-caliber Mammy. We need to acknowledge this in order to mourn the loss of the great performances that never happened. (Note to Hollywood: It's not too late for a Black remix of *Mildred Pierce* starring Taraji P. Henson.) The indignities and struggles suffered by the Black actors and actresses during the making of this movie— segregated restrooms, exclusion from community events, abysmal pay—mirror the indignities and struggles of Black workers in every industry.

Second, it forces us to ask ourselves: Why was this film so wildly popular? Why were White audiences, still reeling from a devastating economic collapse, so hungry for this story about the implosion of the slave-based economy? Why did they find such comfort in the vanilla romance and one-dimensional conflict? Why were they so smitten with the brazenly privileged White characters and the buffoonish Black characters who served them? What's the difference between *Gone with the Wind* and *The Birth of a Nation,* the 1915 film that told a similar story of the "gallant South" during Reconstruction, spurring the resurgence of a dormant KKK? For that matter, what's the difference between these two films and *Forrest Gump,* a famously charming movie in which two White men—one being feeble-minded, the other having lost both legs—are still able to survive and thrive while all the intelligent, able-bodied women and people of color crumble and die?

Lately, I find myself returning to old movies I love with a freshly analytic eye. It bothers me when Black characters seem to be incapable of uttering a single grammatically correct sentence, but I also see how much a talented actress like Hattie McDaniel was able to do within the confines of a painfully limited role. She's there to get paid, every eyelash engaged. She's there to represent, a monument to the struggle, if nothing else.

"But what's the difference between representation and stereotype?" I asked Jacqueline.

"Stereotypes are a category of representation," she said. "Kind of like shorthand."

She recommended Donald Bogle's book *Toms, Coons, Mulattoes, Mammies, and Bucks: An Interpretive History of Blacks in American Films,* which explores the fundamental Black archetypes we're all too familiar with, tropes inherited from literature and minstrelsy, ingrained in everything from opera to advertising.

"Clearly," said Jacqueline, "these are limited roles in so many ways. They don't have the kind of depth of psychology that the White characters have. They don't have the same amount of screen time, but they're doing what they can within those confines—the gestures they make, what they do with their eyes, the inflection of their voices. There's a real mastery that audiences definitely recognized, and it's consistent with the way Black people have found creative practices inside all kinds of systems of restraint."

"Survival," I said, and I could hear my sisters saying, "*Waaaays.*"

When people at the margins create their own images, stories breathe differently. They inhale validation and exhale authenticity. Everyone loves *The Color Purple,* but it always made me profoundly uncomfortable. The Black talent manifested in that film is staggering: Oscar-worthy performances by Oprah Winfrey and Whoopi Goldberg, transcendent music by Quincy Jones, the timeless novel by Alice Walker. But I have to wonder how it might have been different if Steven Spielberg had used the awesome power of his Hollywood influence to place this film in the hands of a Black director.

I can't criticize one thing about *The Color Purple*. It's perfect in every detail. But it's a White man's vision of an intimate Black experience. It doesn't matter that the man himself is brilliant and the vision is beautiful. To me, it feels like that upscale ceramic tile that's made to look like wood. It's gorgeous. It's durable. In many ways, it's *better* than wood. But it ain't wood, and neither is *Amistad*. Then you look at *Schindler's List*—there's wood all damn day. Sometimes you're the right messenger for the moment; sometimes you have to be brave enough to be quiet and carry water for someone else whose voice deserves to be heard.

For me, the bottom line is this: I'm over it. I'm no longer entertained by bleak stories about the victimization of Black people—especially "uplifting" stories about how they grin and bear it. I want to see monuments to the victims of lynching instead of monuments to the lynchers. I want to see stories *by* Black people, not stories *about* us, and I believe it's imperative that Black creators approach those stories with a keen awareness that it's not just Black people watching.

For example, comedian Dave Chappelle's famous hiatus in 2004—that stunning moment when he walked away from a $50 million paycheck—was precipitated, in part, by a sketch in which he played Black Pixie, a tiny blackface bellhop who torments an airplane passenger (also played by Chappelle), singing about fried chicken, tap dancing to banjo music, and calling him "big-lipped bitch" and other epithets, including the n-word and worse. Almost anything Chappelle does is hysterically funny, so this was too. But when he heard a particular White man in the audience laughing a little too hard, Chappelle was stricken with the reality of how the joke actually landed. Fifteen years later, he told the *Hollywood Reporter*: "My head almost exploded."

I've been chided myself, on occasion, by Black people who think I've spoken out of turn. It's not okay to joke about certain things away from the kitchen table. Sometimes Tyler Perry's Madea character is a little too close to the Mammy archetype for my comfort, but Madea made it possible for him to write his own ticket. Now Tyler Perry is blazing trails for other Black filmmakers. His Atlanta studio feels like a bit of FU to old Hollywood. In a way, Madea is a monument to Lena Horne, Hattie McDaniel, and Butterfly McQueen. She's the bridge between *Gone with the Wind* and *Black Panther*.

As Black filmmakers rise, a new mythology rises with them. The story of Wakanda is the story of African colonialism, a Black vision of Black experience. Jordan

THIS IS THE FIRE

Peele's *Get Out* is an inside-out parable about slavery with a subversive side-glance at White liberalism. Spike Lee's controversial *Bamboozled* was a commercial flop in 2000 but achieved cult status as a fresh generation of film buffs dialed into the intensely uncomfortable truth it tells about the pernicious niceties of new-age racism.

———

Just as my mom watched old movies with me, providing context and pointing out impediments, I feel a responsibility to sit with the young people in my own life. I want to talk to them about those archetypes and how they brought us to where we are now, but more than that, I want to listen and learn from them. I want to provide spaces for necessary conversations. We're not at the mercy of one narrow point of view anymore. Whatever the young people in my life are consuming, I don't want them to consume it in isolation.

The interstitial influence of story on societal development is writ large in a movie like *The Birth of a Nation* and quietly footnoted in the form of an Aunt Jemima syrup bottle. It's as tall as a cast-bronze general, as petite as teenage Judy Garland. The same flag that rallied Confederate soldiers to slaughter was emblazoned on the tomato-red roof of Bo and Luke Duke's '69 Dodge Charger, affectionately dubbed "The General Lee."

Jacqueline Stewart laid this profound truth on me: "If we can get people to embrace educating themselves rather than resisting information that can disrupt their pleasure, then I think we would really get to some actual change that we need in our society."

I thought about this statement in the context of my conversation with Reggie Harris and Clayton Wickham and with political analyst Jared Yates Sexton, author of *American Rule: How a Nation Conquered the World but Failed Its People.* Jared talks about foundational myths that have made their way into all aspects of our culture as an "alternate history" created purely for the purpose of subjugating Black people, in society and in their own minds.

"A lot of it was engineered by Woodrow Wilson, who actually was a complete disgusting White supremacist," he told me. "He rewrote American history in this ten-volume *History of the American People.*"

Wilson's slanted mythology of Southern nobility, along with Thomas Dixon's novel *The Clansman,* inspired D. W. Griffith's epic film *The Birth of a Nation,* in which White actors in blackface portray newly freed slaves as a ravening menace to virtuous Confederate men and the lily-White belles they hold dear. It was the first American blockbuster, the first film screened at the White House, and is still lauded as a technological achievement that advanced the art of filmmaking into a new era.

White audiences flocked to see it, gobbling up the lore of the Lost Cause. *The Birth of a Nation* climaxes with a sickeningly prescient vision of Election Day. A phalanx of Klansmen on white horses block a group of shiftless blackface voters from the polls, menacing them until they slink away. Then, with White ascendancy secured, the Klansmen ride off to a wedding, where, in a final feat of cutting-edge movie magic, Jesus Christ himself appears to mingle with the happy guests.

"All of this mythology becomes weaponized and gains a lot of purchase going into World War I," Jared told me, "and that's actually when you start seeing all of these memorials start to pop up."

The Lost Cause mythology seeped into American culture and persists to this day, but an awakening is in progress. The flying of the Confederate flag and hallowing of Confederate "heroes" can no longer be couched as balmy sentiment about the South; it is straight-up White supremacy without borders.

Jared, who lives in Statesboro, Georgia, told me that people entering the courthouse there pass by the bronze statue of a Confederate soldier, who grips his long gun, gaze fixed toward the South, on a twenty-five-foot marble pedestal erected by the United Daughters of the Confederacy in 1909.

"As a White person," he said, "part of my checking of my own privilege is to imagine what it must be like as a person of color to go into one of these courthouses, expecting a fair trial, expecting justice to be done, expecting justice to be blind. And as they walk in, they have to walk past the knowing visage of a Confederate soldier."

I thought of my Black cousins and friends attending Robert E. Lee High School, not only passing under that name to enter each day but wearing the name on hoodies and letter jackets, seeing it imprinted on their diplomas and the dreaded "permanent record."

I asked Jared, "What do you say to folks who claim that these monuments and the Confederate flag are about heritage and Southern pride?"

"It has nothing to do with Southern heritage," he said. "In fact, history shows us that the Confederacy was really terrible to White Southerners. They were held in an oppressive, nightmarish dystopia where they did not have freedom of speech. They weren't allowed to voice opinions that went against the Confederacy. Many of them were punished, hurt, and killed. And by the way, we're talking about the Confederate *battle flag.* We're not even talking about the actual flag of the Confederacy. We're talking about the Confederacy on the move, threatening people and carrying out war. So when you see it around the country, it's not a celebration of a region; it's a celebration of an ideology. It's a celebration that White supremacy still exists within America, even though the Confederacy fell."

"You're White," I said. "You grew up in Indiana. How

do you think of your own identity as it relates to the legacy of White supremacy in America?"

I heard a shadow of sadness when he answered. "I come from a poor family. I love my family dearly. I've seen them become more and more radicalized over the past couple of years. It breaks my heart. I'm seeing people that I grew up with and people that I care for sharing not only White supremacist misinformation, but I'm seeing them become more and more radicalized against African Americans, people of color, and LGBTQ Americans. They're starting to talk about straight fascist ideals."

Oh, yes. There's that now. Facebook: the ultimate myth machine. A bilious bastion of bullshit that divides as much as it connects.

"It's a heartbreaking thing," said Jared. "It's made me reevaluate where I come from and who I was in the past. I tell people constantly that being aware of who you are and your own privilege and what America is—it's exhausting. But there's no other way, because to give up, to just embrace ignorance leads to some really dark places. The past couple of years have been really, really exhausting. But I think necessary."

Exhausting. I hear that. I see it on the streets and in the faces of my colleagues. I feel like we've all aged ten years in a single summer. I hear the weariness in my own voice when I ask a final question:

"Where does this end?"

"I would love to see every Confederate monument either toppled or put into a museum," said Jared. "I mean, we're one of the few countries that actually honors treasonous traitors who have held people in bondage. As long as we're hiding behind this mythologized history, we have no idea where we've been, where we are, or where we're going. We need to not only study the Confederacy, but we need to study the precursors to it, the culture that led to it, which, again, weirdly shadows what's happening now in America."

This, I think, is why some people are so upset to see Confederate flags and monuments fall from grace. The mythology they cling to insulates them from the painful truth about a dark element in our nation's past and in the human heart. To confront that darkness, they would have to accept that they are, in fact, the ones seeking to erase history, continuing a largely successful disinformation campaign that predates the Civil War and Reconstruction. Ironically, in erasing the ugliness of our shared past, they murder the memory of the real people who lived and died—neither villains nor heroes, but actual human beings—who were, in a very real sense, *rescued* by the protesters who tore the statues down.

Whatever good or evil the real Will Wickham did in his life turned to dust the moment his likeness was cast in bronze. Forced to stand on a pedestal he never asked for, he ceased to be a man and became an outsize metal trinket.

Whatever family he had—ancestors who preceded him and progeny who came after—he was estranged from them, suspended between living memory and dead ideals, until his people came for him.

There's a beautiful passage in George Saunders's novel *Lincoln in the Bardo*, a surreal conversation between tortured souls who linger, tethered forever to the monuments and markers in a post–Civil War graveyard: "These and all things started as nothing, latent within a vast energy-broth, but then we named them, and loved them, and, in this way, brought them forth. And now must lose them."

6

About the Benjamins

As the pandemic swept the globe, I found it interesting to observe the ways in which various societies flocked together. The Dutch, for example, who live with longstanding traditions of communal responsibility, were a V-shaped phalanx of geese, streamlining their energy in the most efficacious direction, with only a few stragglers. The United States was a murder of crows, flapping and screeching in a leaderless frenzy, feasting on carrion ideology, pecking at internet roadkill. The resulting deaths rapidly made the United States an object of pity and horror throughout the world. With 4 percent of the world's population, we would soon suffer 25 percent of the global COVID-19 fatalities, faring far worse than many of the nations Trump famously referred to as "shithole countries."

The Trump administration suspended its daily briefings and then resumed them as a one-man show, with Trump speaking in place of medical experts and CDC officials who'd previously stood with him. Predictably, the Trump shtick was littered with fatuous reasoning and blatant falsehoods. Compliance with CDC guidelines was arbitrary, and the CDC itself seemed rudderless and unsure, juggling bedrock integrity with political expediency. In the words of Captain Jack Sparrow: "A dishonest man you can always trust to be dishonest. It's the honest ones you have to watch out for, because you can never predict when they're going to do something incredibly stupid."

The result was a wash of mixed messages and petty grievances that distracted Americans from heated political issues that needed facing and further divided us on the streets.

Businesses continued to reopen in the pleasant shopping district in Sag Harbor, a region redolent with privilege. Out for a morning walk, I stopped by a new boutique selling upscale kitchenware. Cliché as it may be, when life gives me lemons, as it does via potted Meyer lemon trees outside our kitchen door, I make lemonade in my 1960s Sunbeam blender. Citric acid stains a marble countertop, so I appreciate good cutting boards. This little shop had an amazing variety, including the enormous pizza peels you use in an outdoor stone oven.

"That's some cutting board," I remarked, and the clerk glanced up. I smiled behind my mask, wanting to assume that he was smiling too. It's hard to read people these days.

"Sorry, sir," he said. "We're not allowing shoppers inside yet."

"Oh. No problem. I wasn't sure of the rules."

"I mean, I can sell you the cutting board, just..." He glanced toward the door. "You know."

"Sure. I understand."

Passing by the shop again on my way home, I stopped at the doorway to buy two expensive cutting boards. While the clerk rang up the purchase, I noticed a White woman inside shopping.

"What's up with that?" I asked, nodding in the direction of the woman who browsed, a bulky tote dangling on her arm. The clerk tried to tell me the woman was "training," but that's not how it looked. I left with the cutting boards, which now felt ten times heavier and a lot less pretty.

The remainder of my fresh morning energy was consumed with back-and-forth—with Tim, with friends, and inside my own head—over motives, optics, gaslighting, hypersensitivity, and all the possible ways you could deconstruct this incident from various points of view. Because this is what happens when you're shopping while

Black, driving while Black, crossing the street while Black, *breathing* while Black: A White person reacts in a certain way—or did they? *No, no,* they rush to assure you, *you misunderstood.* If you express skepticism—like maybe it isn't really store policy to follow customers up and down the aisles—you're chided for being oversensitive.

"Don't make it about race," we're told. Because racism is so twentieth century.

This sort of gaslighting is exhausting and wears especially thin whenever a Black person is murdered by police, wrongfully imprisoned, or needlessly hassled in a city park. If there's no video, we can pretend it didn't happen, of course, but occasionally, viral photo documentation will trigger momentary outrage. Immediately, a steam valve opens, venting aggregate pressure. Plausible explanations are offered. ("Well, you can't see what happened just before the bystander started filming.") Past wrongs are deconstructed. ("His girlfriend called the police on him one time six years ago.") Fatigue blunts the resolve of Black protesters and the fair-weather support of faux compatriots. ("Can we all just get along?") Hashtags pass in the course of a news cycle or two, and Black shoppers, drivers, pedestrians, and parents return to that unsettled condition of wired watchfulness we all grew up with and consider *normal.*

Think of yourself as a sprinter about to run a race. *Ready?*

You breathe, practiced and confident, feet on the blocks. *SET!*

You rise up, chest tight, every muscle flushed with acetylcholine, every neuron firing. *Wait for it. Wait for it. Here it comes. It's right there . . .*

That hovering edge of hypertension just before the crack of the starting pistol—a perpetual state of *SET!*—that is where I, as a Black man, spend most of my waking hours, and having White people deny that this dynamic exists only serves to pour another tablespoon of fight-or-flight acid into my stomach. No one longs for the bad old days of segregation, but at least there was no pretense about it.

When my mom was growing up in Louisiana, Black families, who paid the same taxes as everyone else, were not allowed in the community center. When integration became the law of the land, city authorities opted to fill the municipal swimming pool with concrete. This was a common occurrence in towns across the United States, not just in the South. White voters went along with it, swayed by fatuous caveats about communicable disease and soft-core tales of priapic Black boys eyeing White girls in varying states of dishabille. Given the choice between spending their tax dollars on an integrated swimming pool or a sunbaked bucket of dry concrete, they chose to swelter through the long summers with no pool at all.

Not rich people, of course, or the upper middle class; they built pools at private clubs or in their own backyards. No, the concrete-filled pools were for working-class Whites, who were then—and still are, in many cases—willing to vote against their own interests in order to ally themselves with a wealthy White upper crust, rather than form logical interest-based alliances with Black people of similar economic circumstances. The reality of the true social order in which they were on an economic par with most Black people—this was an unendurable hair shirt compared to the cheap sateen security blanket of White supremacy. I'm sure they didn't relish being thought of as "White trash," but in their imagination, their "White trash" status could be remedied with the drop of a lottery ball, while Black is forever.

Pool segregation, closures, and privatization offer a distilled example of American racism at its essence: a bitter cocktail of money, sexuality, and power. It had a lingering effect on African American communities long after municipal pools made a comeback in the 1950s and '60s. Open hostility and harassment that sometimes escalated to violence discouraged many Black people from accessing public pools, creating a generational habit of Black families typically swimming far less than their White counterparts or not swimming at all.

A 2008 study by USA Swimming showed that 58 percent of African American children did not know how to swim—twice the percentage of White children—and that Black children were three times more likely than White children to die by accidental drowning. The thought of that feels like a paring knife to my heart. When I was younger, teaching my nieces to swim seemed like one of life's innocent joys. Now I see teaching grand-nephews as a sacred duty.

The cost of racism can be tallied in wasted dollars and wasted lives—lost hours, lost hopes, lost sleep—but the granular truth at the core of our national malady is revealed in that moment when one more mother's child is deprived of his ability to breathe.

The Nighthawk and I are up late, texting back and forth as we watch *Imitation of Life,* a movie based on a novel by Fannie Hurst—the 1934 version with Louise Beavers and Claudette Colbert, though Mom prefers the 1959 remake with Juanita Moore and Lana Turner.

This one is so very good. And so very bad.

The story in a nutshell: A Black woman (Delilah, played by Beavers) shows up at the door of a penniless widow (Bea, played by Colbert) and offers to cook and clean for the White woman and her daughter in exchange for room and board for herself and her own daughter. Bea is over the moon when she samples Delilah's pancakes. Delilah says she intends to take the key ingredient to her grave, but literally two seconds later she voluntarily whispers the secret in Bea's ear, and Bea builds a financial empire selling millions of boxes of "Delilah's Pancake Flour." Meanwhile, the little daughters grow up to be strong-minded women. The White girl lives a charmed life and ends up stealing her mother's boyfriend. The light-skinned Black girl decides to pass as a White woman, which means she must shun her mother, who basically dies of a broken heart.

So many ethical ambiguities; so little time. I would have to write another book to unpack all the angles, so let's just zoom in on two particularly trenchant moments that sum up the kindest possible version of America's economic history:

The first moment is when Bea is launching the company. She gives Delilah full credit for the Black magic pancake flour, cuts her in for 20 percent, and insists on putting Delilah's image on boxes and billboards.

"Delilah, smile." Bea shoves her new bestie in front of a photographer.

Delilah smiles a dignified, close-mouthed smile.

"No, no. You know. *Smile*," Bea urges. "A great big one."

Delilah smiles, affably. But Bea keeps urging until we

see Delilah up in lights on a billboard, mugging a big ol' happy-slappy grin, eyes wide, cheeks like dumplings, clearly ecstatic to be flipping neon flapjacks.

The second moment comes near the end, after a grand party celebrating the success of the company. Delilah is dressed to the nines in party garb, but she's not included in the party, and she's apparently fine with that. As she and Bea hang out afterward, she volunteers to rub Bea's feet. Then the two women bid each other goodnight, and in an iconic shot set up by director John M. Stahl, Bea goes up one flight of the grand staircase while Delilah goes down another. It's a striking image. I truly don't know if he intended to say "How messed up is this?" or if the message is "See how well this works out for all concerned?"

Is *Imitation of Life* a brilliantly subversive statement about racism, sexism, and intersectional alliance? Or is it a conscience-fluffing parable about how *happy* a Black person is under the wing of a benevolent White patron who loves her "like family" and provides beautifully appointed living quarters in a remodeled basement? I can't say what's in another man's heart. I only know I've spent a lot of years trying to climb up that down staircase.

Isabel Wilkerson's groundbreaking book *Caste: The Origins of Our Discontents* lays bare the deeply etched infrastructure of America's caste system as surely as an X-ray held up to the light. Isabel had already won a Pulitzer Prize for journalism and a National Book Critics Circle Award for *The Warmth of Other Suns,* a book about the Great Migration, that watershed era during which six million African Americans moved north to escape Jim Crow laws in the post-Reconstruction South. Isabel told me that while she was writing that book, she came to a profound understanding: the word *racism* did not begin to express the reality of the hierarchy into which every American is born—or into which they immigrate—and within which we all live out our lives, reaping the benefits or suffering the onus of it, regardless of our own best or worst efforts. Race, she told me, is a fairly new idea that dates back only four or five hundred years, to an era of European expansion throughout the world.

"Color is a fact," she said, "but race is a social construct. Caste is essentially the bones, and race is the skin."

In her book, Isabel elucidates three caste systems: those in India, Nazi Germany, and the United States. I know I'm not the only one who resisted the idea of including this country I love in that particular troika. In 1959, inspired by the nonviolent revolution led by Mahatma Gandhi, Martin Luther King Jr. traveled to India. He visited a school for children of India's lowest caste, the Untouchables, now called Dalits. When the principal of the school introduced Dr. King to students as "an American Untouchable," King was taken aback, stung by the appellation. It felt like an insult in the context of a state visit that included public speaking events and dinner with the prime minister.

But as King reflected on the fire hoses turned on peaceful Black protesters, the water fountains and doorways marked "White" and "Colored," the struggle involved in exercising fundamental rights to vote, to drive unmolested, to enter a store without suspicion, or to walk down the street without fear, King was forced to conclude sadly, "I am an Untouchable." Segregation, he realized, was just another word for *caste*, an algorithm that drew hard lines between the indisputably dominant, the utterly subjugated, and a few tiered divisions in between.

India's metric for these classifications is religion. The Third Reich focused on faith, ethnicity, sexual orientation, and other marginalizing factors. The United States keeps it simple with color-coding. What these three caste systems have in common is a need to strictly define how lines are drawn, who belongs where, and what people are willing to do to protect the purity of the dominant caste. I was disturbed to learn that the architects of Germany's Third Reich actually took inspiration from the Jim Crow laws in the United States as they formulated the Nuremberg

Laws, which prioritized racial purity and deemed millions of people—Jews, gypsies, homosexuals, and others—a waste of breath.

Isabel told me she started looking into it after observing the fusion of Nazi and Confederate symbology throughout the White supremacist rally in Charlottesville—the same event where the death of a protester opened the eyes of General Wickham's great-great-great-grandsons. The battle that was supposedly over "history" and "legacy" and the South's noble Lost Cause was quite blatantly about something else altogether.

"The deeper I searched, I discovered these connections that I would never, ever have imagined," said Isabel. "German eugenicists were in continuing dialogue with American eugenicists at the end of the nineteenth century, into the twentieth century, the years leading up to the creation of the Third Reich."

When the Nazis seized power, they invited emissaries from the United States to consult with them on the most efficacious methodology for culling the human gene pool, breeding for "desirable" traits like tall skeletal structure, high intelligence, fair skin, blond hair, blue eyes. The elimination of conversely "undesirable" traits had them scratching their heads: so inconvenient, these curly-haired Jews, fey homosexuals, and swarthy, deviant artists. What to do with such creatures?

As they developed their strategy for Germany's bright Aryan future, the architects of the Nuremberg Laws studied the Jim Crow laws that had so successfully kept Black people subjugated. How clever were these Americans! They'd managed to keep a tight lid on this "undesirable" minority, ensuring their poverty, preventing them from voting, feeding them into the prison labor force, and even openly murdering them—hanging them from trees on blatant display—without upsetting the complacency of the docile White Christian majority.

Isabel Wilkerson lays all this out in the context of rock-solid documentation. This is not revisionist history; this is American history made naked. It's inarguable. And it's disheartening. But at the end of the day, I do believe in the liberating power of truth, and the shift in conversation— the terminology itself—opens a path forward.

"Why say *caste*?" I asked. "Why not just call it out as *racism*?"

"We need new language in the era of upheaval that we live in now," she said. "*Racism* is a term that is so fraught. People have different views on what it means. *Caste* gives us that new language...It frees us, really. It's kind of liberating from the emotion of shame, blame, hatred, and guilt that often is associated with the more familiar language we're accustomed to. It allows us to see the structure of a thing as opposed to the personal stake."

Another way to look at it: White supremacy is hardware. It's machinery. Racism is software. It's programmed.

I weighed that idea back and forth for a few days, test-driving the term *caste-ism* to see how it resonated with people. It felt vaguely sanitized, but in the midst of an acutely troubled summer, a lot of people did find it liberating. It doesn't provide an excuse for someone else's hate; it provides a waste receptacle for our own.

Talking about the "Delilah's Pancake Flour" scenario in the context of a caste system strips away the malice of the autocrat and the indignity of the downtrodden to focus on the inefficacy of the broken system itself. We're not asked to equate Claudette Colbert's sweetly diffident character with cross-burning Klansmen; we're asked to examine the bungled economic machinery that assigns roles based on the least-relevant parameters.

In that context, we see the common ground shared by the homeless Black woman and the indigent White widow, neither of whom would have had a snowball's chance on her own in a White man's economic domain. It makes perfect fiscal sense for these two marginalized people to become allies. So why would they still live and socialize in segregated worlds?

In the context of caste, this relationship is about the Benjamins. "It's not personal, it's business," right? But this *is* personal. Because the only way to sustain a White supremacist business model is to *make it personal* with the visceral doxology of racism.

⸻

Black people were brought to this country for one reason: *money.* Their bodies were a financial commodity used for agricultural labor in the South, factory labor in the North, and domestic labor nationwide. They were, in purely utilitarian terms, *livestock.* The perpetuation of that business model required an elaborate ruse, a social construct that not only codified slavery into law but made it palatable to people who enjoyed thinking of themselves as kind, fair-minded Christians dwelling in the "land of the free."

The architects of racism stripped away opportunities for education and then mocked Black ignorance. They permeated the healthcare system with prejudice and then imprisoned Black people for self-medicating. They burdened Black people with four hundred years of beatdown and then scolded us about pulling ourselves up by our bootstraps.

Visualize that for a moment, if you will—or, better yet, I invite you to give it a try. Squat down right now, grasp your shoelaces and pull. Are you twelve inches off the ground yet? No? Well, then you must be lazy. *Pull harder! Pull yourself up! Come on, bro, you can do it!*

It's ludicrous. And it rings particularly hollow for folks who have no bootstraps to begin with.

"Pulling yourself up by your bootstraps" is not a thing. Because gravity. If someone tells you, "I pulled myself up by my bootstraps," I have news: They didn't. They are simply failing to acknowledge the parents, teachers, social safety net, or educational opportunity that gave them a foothold, a handgrip—some kind of help fused with good luck and canny timing. That's how life works.

I fought hard for every inch of success I've achieved, and there were plenty of people trying to shove me back down or dismiss me, purely because of the color of my skin, but my life was defined early on by people who loved and lifted me. I seek out and forge relationships with people who will continue to love and lift me. I'd be an ungrateful fool if I said I did it myself.

Gravity is a thing. Telling someone to ignore, transcend, or defy the dynamics of gravity does not make gravity not a thing.

Poverty is a thing. Telling someone to ignore, transcend, or defy the dynamics of poverty does not make poverty not a thing.

Racism is a thing. Telling someone to ignore, transcend, or defy the dynamics of racism does not make racism not a thing.

Black people who overcame tremendous obstacles to thrive in the wake of slavery did no less than defy gravity.

They took the meager concessions of Reconstruction and learned to fly. Their resilience, ingenuity, and willingness to rise above grievance served to inspire the first freeborn generation and generations to come, but it posed an existential threat to the citadel of White supremacy, so it also inspired a swift and vengeful backlash.

Wilmington, North Carolina, 1898: Members of the Fusion Party, a political wave that brought together Black legislators and White progressives, ran for state and local offices and won. A White supremacist police force drove them into the woods along with neighbors, family members, and local business owners, then methodically hunted them down and slaughtered 60 to 150 people before installing their own White supremacist candidates in place of duly elected representatives.

Tulsa, Oklahoma, 1921: Affluent Black people prospered in a forty-acre neighborhood known as "Black Wall Street" until they were driven out by White mobs, who burned the economically flourishing area to the ground, killing three hundred, maiming countless others, and leaving ten thousand Black people terrorized and homeless.

Levy County, Florida, 1923: Years of lynchings, beatings, and harassment led to the destruction of the bustling town of Rosewood, where Black neighborhoods were burned and residents massacred.

The list goes on, well into the current century. Black people, regardless of wealth acquisition, are still more likely to die of cancer and COVID, more likely to be gunned down for jogging in their own affluent neighborhood, and more damaged by underlying health issues related to the stress of racism.

Over and over, decade after decade, examples of Black excellence have risen up only to be torn down by violence, barbarism, and soul-haunting ire. Connect those dots to a dead Black man facedown on the pavement, a looted Target burning on the streets of your own city, a polling place closed in your own neighborhood.

Inevitably, for many Black people, the swimming pool effect has come into play; the simple goal of *participation* in the American economy became a demoralizing marathon. As media portrayals of Black communities focus on gangbangers and housing projects, proprietorship, the property ladder, and other avenues through which White consumers naturally engage may seem more and more out of reach. Upmarket goods—technology and toys constantly flaunted in their faces—may seem reachable only through broken glass.

We've all heard the Monopoly analogy circulating since the 1990s: For the first four hundred rounds, while Player A rolls the dice, acquires property, buys railroads, and collects $200 every time they pass GO, Player B does not get a turn. In fact, Player B must provide snacks for Player A, manage the properties, and build the railroads. For the next fifty rounds, while Player A plays on, Player B will theoretically get a turn, but any money they take in will be promptly set on fire. For all subsequent rounds, Player A will play golf while accruing additional wealth through a passive income stream generated by work done by Player B, who will be instructed to pull themselves up by their bootstraps.

What we're left with in the here and now, for many Black people, is the remodeled-basement version of slavery, a 20 percent stake in the prosperous country built by dint of Black industry.

Now, smile. No, smile *bigger*.

In early September 2020, during the Trump town hall on ABC, in reference to the campaign slogan "Make America Great Again," pastor Carl Day asked the president: "When has America been great for the Black people in the ghettos of America? Are you aware of how tone-deaf that comes off in the African American community?"

Trump rebuffed the question with protestations of the good he's done for Black people. He's repeatedly equated his contribution to the well-being of Black Americans

143

with Abraham Lincoln's. I doubt history will remember it that way. I believe that, in the not distant future, this moment in our national adolescence will be viewed with chagrined acceptance of the bald truth — *We screwed up* — and #MAGA will be seen as a cheap cologne fogging the yeasty stench of White supremacist nostalgia.

The reality of racism belies the fond #MAGA daydreams of the innocuous soda jerk at the 1950s soda fountain, where two White bobby-soxers sip a cherry Coke from the same glass. To be truthful with ourselves as a nation, as we must eventually be, we'll have to zoom out and allow our gaze to take in the fire hoses and attack dogs out on the sidewalk. We'll have to stop haggling over the cost of social programs that might benefit people of color and calculate the actual dollar amounts of which they've been robbed.

Barely scratching the surface of the math that needs to be done: assuming fifty-two seventy-hour workweeks per year, even at poverty-level wages — let's say the present-day equivalent of $9 per hour — the average enslaved person would have contributed approximately $32,760 per year in labor to the US economy. Even a brief working life of twenty years adds up to $655,200 per enslaved person. In 1860, the US census reported a total of 3,953,762 people being forced by violence and coercion to work without compensation. Here my calculator fails me. The true value of slave labor in America is literally incalculable. Even if financial records existed, allowing us to make an accurate accounting, it's not possible to identify the people to whom this money is owed.

There is no paying this back. It has to be paid forward in the form of economic opportunity, education, housing, healthcare, and other financial considerations. More immediately, we need to address monetary damages being wreaked on Black families right now: mundane concerns like higher car insurance resulting from racial profiling, higher mortgage rates in redlined neighborhoods, and the lost income that results from racially slanted incarceration.

I reject that old saw "Don't ask the question unless you know the answer." I'm in the business of asking questions to which I don't know the answer, so I've asked countless guests on my show—scholars, historians, activists, executives, rich and poor, old and young, "What about reparations?"

"Oh," they always say, "that's a conversation we definitely need to have."

But we never really have it. A few ambitious theories have been set forth, but I've yet to see the kind of spreadsheet you'd use to plan a family reunion or the pragmatic business plan you'd think through before an IPO. I'm eager to hear the specifics of a credible proposal that might actually gain some traction, but I'm done with the debate over necessity, and I'm definitely not here for the recurring wail about reparations being a "redistribution of wealth."

Redistribution would imply that *distribution* took place at some point. That didn't happen. Larceny happened. Crimes against humanity happened. And not one dollar of "old money" in the United States is untainted by it. Instead of the familiar refrain of Black people lobbying for reparations, I'd like to hear some kind of settlement offer from those who now inhabit the empires built on that mountain of ill-gotten cash.

Economic policy is not my area of expertise; people are. Forgive me if this sounds jaded, but five decades of ass-kicking and keen observation have left me fully informed about what can and cannot be expected from We the White People. Here are three things I've learned about the overwhelmingly White male power structure in the United States:

One: It has the turning radius of a garbage barge. Changes in direction do not happen swiftly or easily, but once made, those changes are not easily or swiftly undone. We know where we stand on that long-promised "arc of the moral universe" that supposedly bends toward justice.

Two: Fear is to be expected, and there will be those

who allow their fear to rule them. There will be a few people who stand outside their mansion, weapons drawn, fingers trembling on the trigger, protecting a way of life they believe is being taken from them, because in their heart of hearts, they know that they have damned themselves with their own Golden Rule: *Do unto others as you would have them do unto you.* The blessing and curse of the American Experience is that, ultimately, none of us will get what we deserve.

Three: Just as the dishonest person can be trusted to be dishonest, the greedy person can be trusted to be greedy, the lazy person to be lazy, and the self-interested soul to brake for self-interest. If the conversation about reparations begins with a conversation about remorse, *forget it.* Why in the name of Ethel Waters would anyone expect *remorse* from people with a history of stealing so much and regretting so little? Remorse is not the American way. Self-interest is.

Americans are a deeply divided people, isolated in conflicting bubbles of information and disinformation. At this moment, our democracy hangs in the balance, our climate is at the brink of cataclysm, and our civil rights are succumbing to chaos. If we hope to make a tectonic shift in how this country functions on a daily household level, we have to take this fight back to where it began: *money.*

And this is where I actually find a shred of hope.

In our broken political machine, it's still possible for a rabidly backward minority to game the system and exert their will, but not in the economy. At the ATM, at the cash register, in the online shopping cart, the majority will rule, because money talks and bullshit walks.

Next time you're watching network television, instead of channel-roving during the commercial breaks, try sitting through a few, and observe the cultural demographics being targeted. Overwhelmingly, you'll see inclusivity, representation, and zealous avoidance of racial, gender, and religious bias. If advertisers know their way around the masses (and trust me, they do), that means the combined marketing demographic—people of color plus White people of conscience—far outweighs the dogged demographic that responds to messages of exclusion and the antiquated vestiges of White supremacy.

Back in 2013, there was a brief online kerfuffle over a Cheerios commercial that featured an interracial couple. General Mills had to shut down the YouTube comments after trolls piled on with racial slurs. The only thing more provocative than this would have been a send-up of the ad featuring a gay couple eating Cheerios, which promptly happened, because let's be real, you can't buy that kind of traction. Overwhelmingly, as the ad went viral, commenters shamed the haters, defended the cherub-level cuteness of the child in the ad, or rolled their eyes at the very idea of such an innocuous vignette being "controversial." In 2020,

I defy you to watch network TV for half an hour without seeing some representation of interracial and/or nonbinary couples. These days, we're frankly surprised if we *don't* see it.

Years before that "controversial" Cheerios ad dropped, we had elected a Black president—the son of a Black man from Kenya and a White woman from Kansas. In 2020 we saw several glass ceilings shattered in one blow by a Black woman of Indian and Jamaican descent who happens to be married to a White Jewish man. I'm a Black man from Baton Rouge engaged to a White man from the East End of Long Island. There's so much racial, religious, geographical, and gender intersectionality going on these days, nobody knows if there's peanut butter in the chocolate or chocolate in the peanut butter. The sliver of our population that actually gives a hoot about that sort of thing is so vanishingly minimal, advertisers don't much give a hoot about them.

Individually and in concert as the overwhelming majority, we need to grow an economic conscience and iron-plate our values with the willful spending—or withholding—of cold, hard cash. In both micro and macro, we must form an unyielding V-shaped phalanx of single-minded consumers who think—no, really *think*—before they feed another dollar into the bloated belly of a White supremacist economy. During the course of the pandemic, we've proven to ourselves and to the powers that be that we are capable of dramatic, lifestyle-level change. We must wield that power, now and forever, as a force for good in the world, and we must fight for political change that makes it possible for all our brothers and sisters to participate.

Here's the macro: Statisticians predict that, in a scant twenty to twenty-five years, the United States will become a minority-majority nation. White people will constitute the largest minority; people of color will be the majority, which places them firmly at the wheel of our economy.

"The stakes are so incredibly high," Isabel Wilkerson said to me, "because we are at a crossroads, a sea change in the demographics of our country. That has consequences for everyone in the entire hierarchy. We're at a turning point in our country's history when it comes to who will we be, what will we be as a country, and how will we move forward."

Here's the micro: I went back to the upmarket kitchenware boutique and returned the expensive cutting boards. With everything going on in the world, I wasn't about to court conflict in my own neighborhood, but I'm done pumping money into businesses that signal an ingrained distrust of non-White customers. I didn't go in with an attitude of castigation or cancellation. I didn't shade the owner on

Twitter or ruin him on Yelp. In all matters of conflict, I strive to find a space of transactional grace, aiming for that negotiable middle ground between "fuck you" and full reparation.

"I need to return these," I said. "They just aren't the right fit for me."

He nodded. "I understand."

We exchanged a few minutes of guarded but neighborly conversation. There was no need for him to continue asserting that the awkward moment had nothing to do with race. Maybe, in his mind, it truly didn't. Maybe, in his mind, the problem is a culture-wide perception that Black customers are oversensitive, having been bombarded since childhood with the message: *We don't want you here.* And maybe he's right. But that doesn't change the bottom line; he didn't make the sale, and making the sale was his objective. He and I share a vested interest in solving this problem.

Changing hearts and minds is a noble ambition, but I'm more interested in changing behaviors. The most civilized way to wage our uncivil war is to make it clear that a price will be paid for racism—and for the *perception* of racism—as it pervades the culture in which we hope to do business with each other. The boutique owner loses sales. The restaurant loses customers. The taxpayer foots the bill for police-brutality lawsuits. These may seem like small moments in a very big picture, but mundane moments of transactional grace eventually add up to movement, and with culture-wide application, movement becomes mainstream.

If we lean in to that dynamic with all the fierceness of the youth in our streets, racism—and the perception of racism—eventually becomes unsustainable.

7

How Change Happens

Tim and I watched the first presidential debate on September 29, 2020, posted up on a hotel bed with our dogs snuggled in the rumpled bedding between us. We were staying at a hotel near the studio in New York, minimizing travel time for the long night ahead. Chris Cuomo and I would be doing the postmortem from midnight until three in the morning.

I don't like to watch debates at the studio. I'd rather see it at home, the way viewers do, but because I had to be on the air that night, we checked in to a hotel. Next best thing. When I watch a debate, I don't take notes. I don't eat. I don't comment. I just take it in. This mess was pretty hard to take. I don't know how people managed it without strong drinks and support animals.

This debate—using that term loosely—was widely condemned as one of the most ugly, mindless happenings in the political history of the United States, a ninety-minute maelstrom of confusion during which Trump bragged and bloviated like a worst-nightmare wedding guest. He interrupted his opponent, Joe Biden, and the moderator, Chris Wallace, more than a hundred times. When it was someone else's turn to speak, he barged in with insults and denials. When it was his turn to speak, he rambled until his two minutes were up, then he just kept carping until he ran out of gas. I'm not qualified to diagnose logorrhea (pathologically aggressive, out-of-control speech), but I can't think of another word to describe it. On a scale of zero to *Great Santini,* it was verbal abuse with a twist of wounded megalomania. Biden emerged the undisputed winner—if there was one—simply by virtue of not embarrassing himself and the nation.

Immediately after the debate, I got on the phone with my producers and started bouncing texts back and forth with Chris Cuomo so we could plan the follow-up programming. Looking for key moments, I gathered incoming reportage from my email and studied the transcripts, which were heavily annotated with qualifiers like "cross talk" and "unintelligible."

We were all nonplussed. This was bizarre, even on the

unhinged continuum to which we'd become accustomed. Twitter buzzed with speculation—ministrokes, Adderall, Alzheimer's, steroids—a lot of theories that came under the umbrella observation "something's wrong with him." But when was that *not* an accurate assessment?

Two days later, everyone was still talking about the "shit show," but we started hearing rumors on a different topic: Hope Hicks, a senior adviser to Trump, was sick and had tested positive for COVID-19. I called a mutual acquaintance.

"It's coronavirus," he said. "It's bad."

I called Jeff Zucker and gave him the information.

He said, "Do you want to go on, or do we wait?"

"I don't want to wait, but I can't reveal my source, and he won't go on record. People are scratching around for it, though. Somebody's going to run with it."

"Okay. Let me call you back."

A few minutes later, he checked back to tell me that the White House correspondents were working on a source who was willing to go on record with confirmation.

This is the challenge of doing actual journalism in the time of Twitter. We don't just pop off with half-baked innuendo like Steve Bannon and the internet troll battalion. We used the inside knowledge to prep while we waited for someone to get a reliable source on record. This happens a lot. The night the infamous *Access Hollywood* "grab 'em by the pussy" tape was made public, I was on the air, stretching—stalling for time—listening to the controlled chaos in my earpiece, trying to imagine how the campaign could possibly spin something this bad. Initially, his supporters tried to sell the "locker room talk" rationalization. Eventually, the Trump campaign issued a perfunctory apology by way of a video that looked like it was shot in someone's basement.

Bloomberg News broke the Hope Hicks story that evening, shortly before we did. She was sick with COVID-19. That's as far as we could go, but we were all thinking the same thing. We were all watching clips of Hicks boarding Marine One, the helicopter that ferries the president and senior staff on short commutes. She ascended the stairs trailing her hand up the rail, followed by Jared Kushner and the rest of the president's closest confidantes, not one of them wearing a mask. I recoiled from the thought of every hand on that stair rail mopping up the sloughing virus like biscuits in gravy.

Someone pulled a file photo of Barack Obama and his staff on Marine One. The helicopter offered extremely close quarters. We were looking at the very real possibility that the POTUS had been exposed and might have contracted a virus that had already killed more than 207,000 people in the United States. Maybe he was already sick.

We had no way of knowing. This administration had all the transparency of a Kevlar vest.

That night, during the *Cuomo Prime Time*/*CNN Tonight* handoff, I said, "We have some breaking news, Chris. What if I told you that the president of the United States is awaiting a COVID test because he may have been exposed? And here's the big thing: he may self-quarantine, he and the First Lady."

"First of all," said Chris, "responsible. That is the protocol. Two: took too long. We should have found out about this on Wednesday night, when they did, because she was in contact with a lot of people, and we have one commander in chief. But why is he waiting on a test now? Why haven't they tested him already? This is the president of the United States. He couldn't get tested any sooner than this?"

As we got into the show, I was interviewing Congressman Beto O'Rourke. We had planned to talk about the outrageous removal of ballot drop boxes in his home state of Texas, a blatant attempt to suppress voting in metropolitan areas heavily populated by Black and Hispanic people, but the topic of Trump and his staff being exposed to COVID monopolized the conversation.

"Look, I hope that Hope Hicks is okay," said O'Rourke. "I hope that the president and his traveling party are okay. I hope that he does not expose anyone else and follows the best public health guidance and medical guidance. I don't think he will. If past performance is a predictor of future performance, then he's not going to. Don, let's remember, this guy is—in large part—responsible for the deaths of nearly 210,000 of our fellow Americans, nearly 16,000 of my fellow Texans, almost 600 of my fellow El Pasoans. We are 4 percent of the globe's population. We are 22 percent of the globe's active cases, almost a quarter of the deaths, and that's not by force of God or Mother Nature, but the miserable leadership of one man—Donald Trump—and every Republican senator who enables him, every Republican governor like Greg Abbott who follows in his footsteps."

I stepped in to clarify that O'Rourke wasn't saying that Trump caused the pandemic, but then I let him roll with the recap while I listened to the production staff in my earpiece.

...confirmation yet? Wait, what? Okay, Don, Trump just tweeted he and Melania are in quarantine awaiting test results...

"While we're concerned about him—as we should be," O'Rourke said, "let's also think about everyone who is sick right now, everyone who has lost a family member, all those who are struggling right now against this pandemic with no help, no strategy, and no plan from the president. For him to know and tell Bob Woodward eight months ago how deadly this virus and this pandemic is— for him to go out publicly and gather people without masks, and to mock those who do wear masks, and to ignore the best public health guidance and thereby infect our fellow Americans, many of whom would end up dying from COVID-19—yes, he bears responsibility for many of those deaths."

My producer was telling me to break away, but I let O'Rourke finish his thought before I said, "Okay, I need you to stand by. I'm sorry, Congressman. I have to get some breaking news right now. I want to go to CNN's Kaitlan Collins on our breaking news. As I understand, Kaitlan, the president is going to quarantine, is that correct?"

"Yes. This is notable because this is not something the president has done when anyone else around him has tested positive. Don, I don't know exactly what this means, but it is telling that the president says they took a test tonight, they don't have the results—still—at almost eleven o'clock, over an hour after the president first said they were waiting on the results. And we know the White House has the fifteen-minute tests at their disposal. It's what they use to test people every single day."

This is where responsible journalists walk a very thin high wire. We have to be circumspect, lead with facts, and avoid speculation, but it wasn't hard to do the math: if the president had tested negative, they would have immediately rushed to say so. Keep in mind, this is someone whose only real success in life was a reality TV show that someone else wrote for him. He'd surrounded himself with people who understand the key elements of reality TV: manufactured conflict, scripted relationships, and carefully timed reveals. Suck people in and keep them watching.

It hurts to think about how he could have applied this formula to the pandemic. I mean, you want drama? Here it is on a silver platter. He could have run with it, set a sterling example, showcased the scientists and caregivers, and rallied the nation to heed our better angels. He could have made himself a hero and potentially saved countless lives. Even at this moment, he could have pretended this brush with death had transformed him into a better man.

But that was not in the script. In this administration, as in reality television, ratings mattered above all else. They seemed to care more about being right than being truthful.

Over the next two hours, while social media ran wild with supposition, we stretched what we had, waiting for official word from the White House. I usually go off the air at midnight. That's when CNN operations switch from the New York studio to master control in Atlanta, replaying Anderson Cooper's show from earlier in the evening. MSNBC does the same thing, replaying Rachel Maddow, while Fox reruns Tucker Carlson. In that hour, not one of the major news networks was broadcasting live, so if you knew we were all hanging from a piano wire, waiting for a story to break, that's the precise moment you'd be able to screw us all over. Jeff and I weren't about to fall for that. I stayed on the air, stretching, staying true to the tightrope, listening to my earpiece while the control room hustled to line up whatever guests they could roust out of bed.

At 1:00 am, my producer signaled for me to sign off. Within seconds of the switch, Trump pulled the trigger on a tweet confirming that he and the First Lady had tested positive for COVID-19. I hadn't even left the studio. I got a text, saw the tweet, and speed-dialed Jeff.

"POTUS and FLOTUS are confirmed positive. Get me back on."

Control whiplashed back to New York, but just as I hit the chair, rigged with my earpiece and mic, I heard an announcement over the building's PA system—something about a damn fire drill, of all things.

"You will be hearing alarms for the next several minutes…"

"Aw, *hell,* no!" I unplugged and ran out, shouting down the hallway to the security guards. "Stop the drill! Stop the drill! We're on the air!"

Dodging back into my little studio, I grabbed my earpiece and mic.

Okay, we're—no, we don't have the teleprompter… no, just the tweet. Don, you'll have to wing it…Tell Don to go…

"Go to what? I can't hear you."

It didn't matter. I was on. I had to start talking. Facts first. Facts first.

"The president of the United States has tested positive for COVID-19."

A virus invades your body. Fever rises to burn the aggressor off. Your body's autonomic response is an attempt to quell the fever. You sweat. You shake. The intractable virus doubles down. The fever burns hotter, setting off your body's built-in fire alarms. Your head pounds in a rhythm with your quickened pulse. You reach for something to artificially force the fever down— ibuprofen, cool compress—though you know this will do nothing to kill the virus. That's not your goal. Your goal is to return to a comfort level that allows you to go about your business. Your goal is the sustainably numb coexistence of virus and host. And that might work for a while. But as long as the virus survives, the fever will continue to sear and spike, burning higher and hotter in an effort to eradicate the real problem: the virus.

Now your body's self-defense mechanisms kick in with a vengeance. You vomit up everything, including vital stomach acids. Proteins break down as dehydration reduces blood volume. Your gut fails. Your brain falters. Cells in your liver and kidneys forget their function and abandon their purpose. Your body convulses, at war with itself. This is going to play out one of two ways: either your body will eradicate the virus, or your body will burden itself with a flailing response of ever-increasing lymphocytes, snot, and spontaneous combustion until it shuts down.

A virus doesn't destroy you; it goads you to destroy yourself.

Racism, our national malady, is a contagious assailant we've hosted for four hundred years. Many who consider themselves "woke" are still part of the problem. They mask the deeply embedded proclivities of racism in a well-intentioned effort to keep it from spreading, but when it comes to actually solving the problem, they're no more helpful than the denialists, who claim the real problem is the cleansing fever burning in our streets. We are all vulnerable to the cascading systemic effects of this disease. Even within the Black community, not one of us is immune.

Growing up down South, I came of age under the convoluted hierarchy of colorism that pits Black people against each other and plays into the hands of White supremacy. I saw the way this caste-within-a-caste system was parsed to the smallest fractions and used to divide communities and even families. I heard the way pejoratives invented for the benefit of White folks invaded the mouths of Black people, who picked up on language with a willing sort of Stockholm syndrome. People who were three-quarters Black were *griffes*. *Mulattoes* were half Black, *quadroons* a quarter, *octoroons* an eighth, and so on, down to the one-sixty-fourth Black *sangmelee*.

These anachronistic terms offend our ears now, but the old "brown paper bag test"—a sliding valuation of skin tone versus stature—still whispers in the subconscious mind of the job interviewer and the job applicant, the loan officer and the loan applicant, the teacher and the student, the cop and the citizen. We'd like to think we've moved beyond all that. But have we really? Political correctness usually binds the tongue, but that's the easy part. That's the low-grade fever remedy that allows us to go about our business.

I believe we could be, at long last, witnessing the death throes of White supremacy in the United States. The sheer impracticality of White supremacy as a business model is at critical mass, but this invasive ideology will not go gently. We're past the point of low-grade remedy; 2020 has brought us to the shivering brink of convulsion. Peace, equilibrium, and the intelligent pandemic response that could have and should have happened are all casualties of our inane uncivil war. We are killing each other, killing people we love, killing *ourselves*.

The Horace Wilkinson Bridge spans the stretch of the Mississippi River that rolls, ponderous and brown, between Port Allen and Baton Rouge. It was built in the 1960s, but people still refer to it as the "new bridge" so as not to confuse it with the older, more decrepit O. K. Allen Bridge.

"The old bridge" was named after Governor Oscar K. Allen, who was celebrated in a Lead Belly tune about the release of almost four hundred mostly Black prisoners from Angola, the state prison, in 1932. This was not an altruistic or egalitarian gesture. There was a Depression in full swing, and too many mouths to feed at Angola. Apparently, these men posed no danger to society. They'd mostly been penned up for petty hand-to-mouth misdemeanors and nebulous "stepping out of line." When the forced labor that the state got out of these men became less valuable than the modicum of food and supervision they required, they were released. Governor Allen signed off on it, so—okay, O. K.—give the man a bridge. It's a lot more useful than a bronze statue.

The night before Leisa's funeral, on our way to her wake, Mom and Yma and I sat on the old bridge in a rented car on our way to the funeral parlor where Leisa's body was laid out for family and friends. The viewing of the body is not exclusive to Black funerals, and it's usually a big deal. It's not about saying goodbye; you know the soul has flown. It's about accepting this new reality, the cold flesh and dry bone of what's happened.

Traffic crawled, stop and go, like an inchworm. I craned my neck, trying to find some explanation for the standstill. Red and blue lights flashed between the iron beams up ahead. Something big, a truck of some kind, was sprawled across the lanes. There was no turning around, no backing up, no going forward. I kept checking the time on my phone, looking at the arrival time on Google Maps. We'd left with plenty of time, we thought. Now it looked like we were going to be late.

"No," I said. "No, no, no. This is not happening right now."

"It's the weekend," said Yma. "Why would it be like this?"

"It just is," said Mom. She stared out the window, eyes vacant. She shrugged. "What are you going to do?"

In the days since Leisa's death, Mom had been smoking like a chimney, twitchy with exhaustion, addressing all the details with a wired frenetic energy. Now a terrible calm settled on her. It killed me to see my mom, this force of nature, looking so vanquished.

"I used to cross this old bridge every morning," she said. "For college. And later, when I was working for your father and we were all staying at Mame's."

Remember, in the 1960s, my father was Black Perry Mason, and Mom was Black Della Street. Those were the days when famed civil rights attorney A. P. Tureaud battled the cases that brought incremental progress for Black people, ramming his head against a brick wall of Jim Crow edicts and the more insidious unwritten rules of bigotry. Tureaud fought and won the case that made it possible for his son—and my father's only son—to attend LSU. He represented the NAACP in a lawsuit that ended a century of segregation in New Orleans. He waged a five-year battle to desegregate city buses in Baton Rouge. My father was one of four young lawyers on that legal team—at a time when fewer than 1 percent of practicing lawyers were Black, and people weren't exactly naming bridges after them, if you know what I mean. I wish I'd known when he was alive what a badass he really was, because ever since I learned about it, I've felt a bit of that badass in myself.

I remember crossing the old bridge throughout my youth, even though there was a better way—the *new* bridge—built for fast cars and eighteen-wheelers instead of milk wagons and Model Ts. The new bridge didn't lead as quickly from where my dad lived in Baton Rouge to Mame's part of Port Allen. We had a perfect balance back then: Mom and Leisa up front, Yma and I in the back. Two and two. If you had only one person in the backseat, people called that "riding nigger"—a phrase I vaguely understood to mean *wrong* for reasons that required only that word as explanation, maybe because it conjured images of an unfortunate soul in the back of a police car. I tried not to think about that now that Leisa was gone and we were a lopsided party of three. The rental car felt as cavernous as a 747.

"I pretty much started my life going back and forth on this bridge," I said.

Yma nodded. "Me and Leisa too. I remember learning to drive here."

"Yeah, you'd get nervous as you came closer, and it seemed so narrow, but then you'd get out over the water and feel like you're flying."

"But if the train passed down the middle," said Yma, "the whole thing would be vibrating and shaking."

"You'd feel it sway and think, *Help me, Jesus! It's gonna fall.*"

"This bridge used to be narrower," said Mom. "They expanded it."

We started telling stories, recalling all the good reasons we had for coming and going back and forth, waxing philosophical about the role this bridge had played in our lives. It connected our family to my father and, later on, to my stepfather. It connected each of us—Mame, Mom, Leisa, Yma, and me—to our larger purpose in a bigger world. As I got older, the new bridge meant freedom to me. It meant meeting friends downtown and listening to music as I cruised over the river on my way to school, on my way to work, and finally on my way out of this sleepy Southern parish.

The old bridge was a symbol of the way things changed as the story of our lives unfolded within the greater story of Louisiana. Down below us, all along the riverbank, were the last vestiges of the plantation culture that had sprung up and thrived along this great waterway. Elderly

Black folks still inhabited some of the dilapidated shotgun houses, but the modern city of Baton Rouge was encroaching. Gentrification was coming, and I'm one of those who tends to say, "Let it come." Let the old plantations turn to dust and disappear like the old O. K. Allen Bridge. Isn't that the way progress works? One day, you look up to find something you thought was ironclad is gone, and a better way has replaced it.

I was surprised to hear my mom's throaty laughter in the dark beside me.

She said, "I remember one time we were on our way back from your dad's, and you were just looking at me funny, and I said, 'Why are you staring at me like that?' And you said, 'How can you see to drive? There's something wrong with your glasses. The lens is missing.' And I said, 'No, it's just clean so you can't see it.' I went to show you and poked myself in the eye. The lens was out."

Yma and I cracked up at that, laughing the kind of deep belly laughter you so desperately need when you're on your way to do the hardest thing you've ever had to do. We sat there for what seemed like a long time, talking and laughing.

It was a blessing, honestly. A reprieve. It placed Mom and Yma and me close together in the dark, forcing us to just be together, love each other, and accept that sometimes, you think you have to be somewhere, but the universe has other ideas.

* * * *

The world is full of seemingly uncrossable divides, micro and macro, personal and political. Americans didn't invent festering hate or fresh grievance. That shit is older than Longfellow's "forest primeval."

Throughout history, plenty of other societies—some of them far more messed up than our own—have figured out ways to effect sweeping cultural, legislative, and economic changes. They figured out ways to build and traverse bridges between what was and what needs to be. With the technology and resources at our command, we should be *better* at it than they were. We have no excuse not to be!

Just unpack this with me for a minute: *How does change happen?*

Anger makes change happen. Rage. Desperation. It would be disingenuous to deny that violence is part of that. Push people far enough and they reach a tipping point where they can't take it anymore. In 1789, the common people of France couldn't take another year of hunger, poverty, and imprisonment. In July, rebels stormed the Bastille and organized the National Constituent Assembly, whose first order of business was to abolish feudalism, a six-hundred-year-old caste system left over from the Dark Ages.

That October, some twenty years before the German

Coast Uprising, one woman in a Paris marketplace began banging a drum, and the women around her fell in step. They took bread and weapons and kept marching, and by the time they reached the Paris city hall, they were ten thousand strong. What began as an impromptu protest ended up dislodging the monarchy, forced the king to get on board with sweeping governmental reforms, and forever established the awesome power of the people.

Solidarity makes change happen. In modern times, nonviolent civil resistance has achieved lasting reforms more successfully than violence. When I was a kid, the seemingly impenetrable Iron Curtain surrounded Eastern Europe. The United States and the Soviet Union were entrenched in an unwinnable Cold War, and most people couldn't imagine any meaningful shift in that balance short of full-on *Dr. Strangelove* bomb-jockey insanity. In the late 1960s, a Polish shipyard electrician, Lech Wałęsa, began agitating, talking about democracy, and winning people over to the idea that if they set aside their differences and banded together with a common purpose, they could overturn the authoritarian government. By the time I graduated college, communist Poland was over, the Soviet Union had collapsed, and Wałęsa was a Nobel Peace Prize laureate and president of Poland.

Compassion makes change happen. Under apartheid, the South African government decreed that since Black people need not be educated for anything other than menial service to White employers, all instruction should take place in either English or Afrikaans—"the language of the oppressor," according to Bishop Desmond Tutu. In June 1976, thousands of Black high school students marching through the streets of Soweto in peaceful protest were met with unmitigated police brutality that left several hundred dead and over a thousand injured. Violent anti-apartheid protests had been happening for decades; this march accomplished what violence never could. Seeing televised images of children massacred in the name of "law and order," White South Africans finally began wrapping their heads around the idea that apartheid and human decency were not compatible, and despite their fears, a lot of them were willing to at least keep decency on the table as an option.

Catholic schools stepped outside the law to end segregation and welcome Black students. Journalists covered and amplified the horrors of colonialism. White people in South Africa began voting for political platforms that promised an end to apartheid, and people of all races all around the world began to condemn and sanction South Africa, demanding the release of Nelson Mandela and other political prisoners. It didn't happen overnight, but Black people in South Africa eventually won the right to vote, and Mandela was elected president.

Vision makes change happen. Every potent agent of

change, good or bad, has in common a clarity of vision that makes it possible for people to see and believe in a better way. Human nature hungers for vision. People are willing to live and die for it. When the vision of a better way is missing, failure of imagination rushes in to fill that void with fear, making it possible for anti-visionaries to bring out the worst in us.

Jesus inspired unwavering disciples. Martin Luther King knew how to work an audience. Joan of Arc erased fear from the hearts of an army. In 61 AD, a deposed Celtic queen named Boudica, using only the power of skilled rhetoric, articulated a vision that rallied the British citizenry. She led them into the ancient city of Londinium (now London) and burned that joint to the ground. It's one of the only campaigns that even came close to beating back the Roman Empire, which wasn't toppled, but it was changed.

Look, each of these examples is the epitome of "long story short"; I encourage you to read more about all of them. If you want a real primer in change-agenting, read *Across That Bridge: A Vision for Change and the Future of America* by John Lewis or check out the revolutionary reading list in the appendix at the end of this book.

We're closer than you think—closer than a lot of people even want to think, because most people find change so very frightening. I've seen anger manifested in the streets.

Solidarity crystallized and took a knee. Compassion came up in a groundswell of emotion, transcending all the usual barriers.

Vision is all that's left. And that's where I get scared.

Trump came to power in 2016 brandishing his clarity of vision like a school shooter brandishes an AR-15: with singular intent, zero regard for human life, and absolute immunity to shame or reason. He was the son and the father of unscrupulous users, the celebrity of *The Celebrity Apprentice*. He wore his TV persona like a thick band of fat in a Trump steak. In my lifetime, I have not seen a competing vision that has a fraction of his simple-minded wallop, probably because no competing visionary is brazen enough to pull the rip cord on every falsehood and conspiracy theory that might advance their cause. A troll army coalesced around him and sucked in enough "just folks" to intimidate political adversaries.

Trump's campaign of uniquely American racism, uniquely American greed, and the counterfeit virtue of self-importance will continue to embolden White supremacy in the United States for decades to come. You can't unbake that cake. We'll see middle school bullies walking with his stiff-chinned gait and hear his toxic bravado from the mouths of his doppelgängers—both male and female. Long after the man himself is gone, the fetid stench of Trumpism will linger, and the emboldened thrust of that code will always be about who's sitting up front and who's riding nigger.

On Saturday, October 3, 2020, at the Kwik Chek convenience store in Wolfe City, Texas, Jonathan Price, a 31-year-old Black man, witnessed the assault of a young woman and intervened to help her. This is the kind of man Price was, his family said, and his old high school football coaches agreed. He was well known in his community as an affable, upstanding guy. A clerk inside the store also saw the "possible fight" and called the police. By the time the patrol car rolled up, the altercation was over.

"Hey, man. Ya doing good?" Price greeted the officer, 22-year-old Shaun Lucas, and offered his hand with a broad smile.

Lawyers for Lucas said later that the young officer thought Price was reaching for his taser. He declared his intent to detain Price, and when Price tried to walk away, Lucas ended up shooting him dead. But no one started any fires for Jonathan Price. No woke masses marched— *say his name, say his name*—and, to be honest, I don't even recall most of the main news outlets covering it. When George Floyd's name first echoed through the tear gas, we all said, "This time, yes, this time feels different."

A scant four months later, we were back on the same tired carousel.

Weeping.

Rage.

Blame.

Promises.

Complacency.

The story of Jonathan Price's murder caused less than a ripple on the reservoir of 24-7 coverage about Trump's COVID-19 diagnosis, Trump's appearance, Trump's feeble gait, the bellicose assurances and freakish makeup in Trump's weird little "proof of life" videos posted to Twitter and Facebook.

Less than two weeks after he tested positive for COVID-19, Trump was back in his element, sucking all the air from the room, boasting about his ability to dominate the virus by virtue of his being "a perfect physical specimen." Within days, he was back on the campaign trail, speaking to a mostly unmasked audience in Sanford, Florida, a five-minute drive from the sidewalk where seventeen-year-old Trayvon Martin was murdered on his way home from a quick trip to the convenience store for a bag of Skittles. This was the community that stood up for the murderer, the pool from which a jury of his peers were selected and set him free. Trump knows how to work that audience. He went home to his people, shrilling his racist dog whistle, wheedling, "Suburban women, please like me! I saved your damn neighborhood."

I spoke with Jordan Klepper, a contributor to *The Daily Show,* who's made it his mission to attend Trump rallies and interact with rally-goers over the past five years. There are too many absurdly incongruous exchanges to choose from, but here's one of my favorites:

KLEPPER: Are you in a better place than four years ago?

TRUMP SUPPORTER: Absolutely. Absolutely.

KLEPPER: Is America in a better place than it was four years ago?

TRUMP SUPPORTER: I believe, absolutely.

KLEPPER: We have higher unemployment, we have two hundred thousand people dead due to COVID, and we have riots in the streets.

TRUMP SUPPORTER: Yes. Let me tell you this much. *I* am doing much better. I am literally making four times as much as I was making when Obama was president.

KLEPPER: What do you do?

TRUMP SUPPORTER: I work for a debt relief company.

I asked Jordan what, if anything, had changed at these rallies between 2016 and the current election season.

"There is still an energy there," he said. "That's undeniable. There was four years ago. But if you're going to the Spin Doctors for the first time—they were exciting their first time out. If you're still going to Spin Doctors concerts four years later, you might be excited about the hits, but you've heard that song over and over again."

Racism was high on the list of Trump's greatest hits. It was no longer a matter of politics; it was about identity.

The goal of war-making is not to kill people; the goal of war is to control people and claim territories. The goal of war is to intimidate to the point where it's possible to enforce the will of the winner, and the "good" or "bad" side of any war is entirely subject to which side you're on. Everyone imagines they're the good guy; no one hears the language of the oppressor coming out of their own mouth. All of us who grew up watching the *Star Wars* franchise want to see ourselves as the Jedi, but real-life conflict and morality are not so cut-and-dried.

If anything good can come from war, it's that no one will ever understand the imperative of peace better than the fatigued people of a war-torn nation. These are people who have been forced to accept that their society is subject to turbulence, their culture is destined to evolve, and their home is vulnerable to fallout. War is a powerful catalyst for change, and like it or not, it's up to We the War-Weary to steer that change in the way of benevolence, progress, and peace.

In order to move forward, we must form unshakable coalitions of marginalized people. How are we still unable to process the reality that racism, misogyny, and homophobia go hand in hand? How do we not see each other as allies in our mutual struggle for equality, pay parity, and a universally applied code of justice? Imagine the life-changing, world-shifting power of solidarity between people of color and people of conscience.

It's time to exit the Oppression Olympics and get over our what-aboutism. Black brothers and sisters, please contemplate the fact that, in the White Man's World, the chattel status of White women goes back thousands of years before the slave trade. And the word *fag* originated with the burning of homosexuals at the stake as far back as Bible times. There's work to be done in the Black community, particularly among Evangelical Christians, who treat LGBTQ brothers and sisters with the same vitriol and discrimination they themselves are complaining about. That said, if we keep the conversation in the here and now, eye on the ball, we must recognize that Black men live every day with the threat of imprisonment and police brutality swinging over our heads like a sledgehammer.

Our most immediate action has to benefit those most immediately at risk, and all of us in turn must do what we can to protect someone other than ourselves.

* * * *

I felt a slight breeze of progress in October 2020 when the White police officer who killed Jonathan Price was charged with murder in less than forty-eight hours. There was none of the usual feet-dragging—weeks of "administrative leave while we sort this out" or months of "examining the facts carefully" followed by a soul-crushing dismissal. In this small Texas town that was 71 percent White, we saw a distinct shift of attitude at every level of response, undeniably because of a shift in public awareness and tolerance.

The following week, Amy Cooper, the White woman who called 911 when a Black man asked her to leash her dog, was charged with falsely reporting an incident in the third degree. Manhattan district attorney Cy Vance issued a statement pledging a commitment to "safety, justice, and anti-racism" and said: "Amy Cooper engaged in racist criminal conduct when she falsely accused a Black man of trying to assault her in a previously unreported second call with a 911 dispatcher. Fortunately, no one was injured or killed in the police response to Ms. Cooper's hoax. Our office will pursue a resolution of this case which holds Ms. Cooper accountable while healing our community, restoring justice, and deterring others from perpetuating this racist practice."

Obviously, the big-picture goal is to live in a society

where we don't have to equate police response with the potential for Black people to be injured or killed. But this is a step in the right direction. I'm willing to accept the DA's commitment at face value, but that doesn't mean we don't keep the fire hose on the fire. We must engage with and advance meaningful, well-organized, nonviolent activism, supporting it with our presence, voices, and resources.

Vote.

March.

Donate to well-researched causes.

Educate yourself and think before you tweet.

Keep your eyes open and cameras at the ready, recognizing how important it is to focus the conversation with images that document incidents of racism and provide incontrovertible evidence for those seeking justice. ("Receipts or it didn't happen," right?)

Listen thoughtfully and speak mindfully, with the purpose of healing.

Continue on, and keep continuing on when you're tired, when it seems there's no point, when the voices of hate and bullshit blather over you—continue on. Because no specific moment, no single election, no particular situation is going to make or break this effort. The moment you're in now is the moment that matters.

Perhaps the one thing none of us truly had the ability to grasp as we were walking through the thick forest of 2020 is how little this election mattered in the big picture.

If you study history's examples of societal change—from the Magna Carta to MLK—you'll see that it was never about principalities or powers that be. It was about people, and people grow. People change. Regimes, religions, and old-thinking governance might be able to keep a lid on it for a while, but we are human, and human nature is to evolve. We must hold on for the evolution of ourselves. I promise you, it's inevitable. It's already happening.

Tensions were high in the run-up to the 2020 election. Joe Biden was being shopped as the egalitarian unifier who would heal the sundered soul of our nation. Donald Trump marketed himself as a blast furnace of undaunted nationalism, stoked by the desperation of his ardent base. The contrast was as classic as a midcentury comic book. On November 1, shopkeepers in Seattle and Chicago started boarding up their windows, certain that there would be mayhem no matter which side won. Chris Cuomo and I were scheduled to bring our Rowan & Martin routine to the late-night election coverage, knowing that this wouldn't be the election-night coverage we were used to.

Because Trump had disparaged early voting and cast doubt on mail-in ballots, most of his base was expected to vote in person on Election Day. Because Biden espoused strict adherence to COVID-19 guidelines, his people were expected to vote primarily by mail. The effect, because of the order in which votes were counted, was an initial onslaught of votes for Trump that was eventually overcome by the slower but steadier influx of votes for Biden. The outcome of this election was not the "blue wave" many had hoped for. Trump lost the electoral college in a landslide, but the margin of victory was narrow in several states. Spastic efforts to overturn the election results—foiled by courts at every level—made it possible for Trump to continue fundraising long after the election was over, feeding the delusions of his myopic faithful who didn't want to accept the results.

As the dust settled, a lot of people expressed shock and horror to find that seventy-four million Americans still voted for Trump after he revealed himself to be an incompetent, careless despot. But I was not surprised. I suspect you'd have a hard time finding any Black person who is surprised to find that peeling back one layer of racism in this country always reveals another layer underneath. But that layer is still a crucial step forward. You never know how deep racism goes until it's tested. This was the semester exam we've been working up to for five years. Teacher posted the results on America's classroom door. We see who everyone is and where they stand. If you didn't know, well, now you know.

Our country's bloody beginning has been, is being,

and will inevitably be overwhelmed by an inexorable tide of progress. It's never enough. Progress is imperfect. We should consider ourselves defeated only if we fail to find hope in it.

———

Not long ago I learned through DNA testing that, on my mother's side, I'm the direct descendant of a slave called Catherine and a plantation owner named James C. Woods, the man who owned her. Following that thread of my lineage five centuries back, through the Scottish moors into the mist of history, I was surprised to find an element of pride and fascination I would not have expected. I thought about the overwhelming likelihood that many— if not most—African Americans share some White lineage. Our ability to reconcile that within ourselves may be the key to our nation's ability to confront the painful aspects of our past.

I was born in 1966, one year before the United States Supreme Court announced their ruling in *Loving v. Virginia* striking down laws that prohibited interracial marriage. According to a 2017 study by the Pew Research Center, in 1967, approximately "3 percent of all newlyweds were married to someone of a different race or ethnicity." By 1980, that ratio had risen to 7 percent. In 2015, it was 17 percent, contributing to the overall number of interracial couples who'd already been together for years or even decades, a total of more than eleven million people, or roughly 10 percent of all married couples. The percentage of Black people married to someone of a different race or ethnicity has risen from 5 percent to 18 percent in the past thirty years. Meanwhile, the percentage of multiracial children in the United States has risen by 32 percent, making multiracial children the largest ethnic demographic under 18 years of age.

Tim grew up in an environment with very little diversity, but his family was unconditionally supportive when he came out, and they welcomed me with open arms. Questions about our interracial relationship were more likely to come from gay friends, and for most of them, the real shocker is that I was once a Young Republican.

It's hard for children of the Obama era to wrap their heads around it, but when I was a child, Republicans were the pro-integration, pro-ERA, pro-choice progressives down South. Before it was the party of Barack Obama, the Democratic party was home to "Dixiecrats" like George Wallace, the Alabama governor, who promised no Black child would enter a White school so long as he had strength to stand in front of the schoolhouse door. Wallace started voting Republican not long after I abandoned the "party of Lincoln," which had embraced Reaganomics, fundamentalist Christianity, and a virulent homophobia that turned lethal with the onset of the HIV/AIDS crisis.

These days, like Dr. Martin Luther King during his lifetime, I don't affiliate myself with any political party.

Political parties de-align and re-align in a continuing cycle. Party loyalty is not a virtue. It requires voters to suspend both conscience and critical thinking. This is what makes unblinking party fealty so nonsensical, but it's also how I know that we are all capable of evolution.

Tim says the differences between our race, age, and background keep us asking, listening, and learning about each other.

"We might have an awkward conversation," he said recently. "It might even turn into an argument, but we know where we're both coming from. I'm a better person because of it. Without it, I wouldn't address most of these topics."

I'd like to think that same dynamic applies to the way we engage with the world around us. There are times when the conversation gets strained, but if we arrive with love and leave with greater understanding, the national conversation about race and racism might calm down enough to take a more practical turn.

Tim and I don't spend a lot of time debating the conflicting viewpoints of Booker T. Washington and W. E. B. Du Bois; we go back and forth about what to binge-watch and whether Tim should get an equal say about it when we both know he's going to fall asleep within the first three minutes.

"Weekend highs and lows. Go," he'll say to me on a

Sunday night, and I have to come up with something relatively romantic about the simple pleasures of the life we share.

"Your homemade cider."

"It was watery," he said, "but flavorful."

"The story of our lives."

We talk about the challenges of making a family that brings together two driven professionals, three emotionally complicated dogs, a vintage station wagon full of kids, parents, siblings, and extended family, plus a sprawling network of friends we never see enough of. We talk about the future far more often than we talk about the past. We talk about things that bind us together far more often than we talk about things that drag us apart. That's key to who Tim is, key to why I love him. I look forward to a day when I'll turn to him and say, "Decade highs and lows. Go."

In every beautiful moment, there is some element of pain, and in every painful moment, there is some element of beauty. That's what makes love such fertile ground for change. Everyday interactions—shared families, shared children, shared lives and love—these are the stone and timber with which we build the bridge.

I met Tim's nephew Henry on Easter Sunday in 2017. Henry was a cheerfully determined preschooler. He wanted me to go on the trampoline with him, and I foolishly did. I threw my back out, and I swear I still feel occasional muscle twinges from it, but Henry and I were partners in crime from that day to this. He wants to come over and hang out with us. He begs me to heat up the pool, show him my hoverboard, and let him steer the boat.

My grand-nephew Cairo, who is the same age as Henry, refers to Tim as "Uncle Don's husband." Henry refers to me as "Uncle Tim's friend." It occurs to me that the two of them will, from their earliest memories, be part of a family in which not everyone has the same color skin, and in which the very definition of *family* is fluid. I wonder about the difference that will make in the way they think about people.

I'd like to say that I find a wellspring of hope there, but I also wonder how their paths will diverge as they grow up in a world that tells them in not-so-subtle ways that a Black man is suspect and merits separation in ways that are more than skin-deep. In recent years, we've heard the president of the United States call Black football players "sons of bitches" and tell Black congresswomen to "go back to your own country." This administration will someday fade from memory, but those words were hammered home. You can pull the nail out, but the hole is still there.

Tim and I have wondered about how and when we

should talk to Cairo and Henry—and to our own kids someday—about race and racism, so I asked Beverly Daniel Tatum, former president of Spelman College and author of the book *Why Are All the Black Kids Sitting Together in the Cafeteria? And Other Conversations About Race*. She said, "You can start talking with your children about race and racism, and should, when they are toddlers, because the ideas that they have about race are being shaped from birth, really. By the time a child is talking—2 years old, let's say—that child can be expressing opinions about skin color."

She told me that kids Henry's age express and internalize messages and questions about skin color and that her own 3-year-old had asked her, "Is my skin brown because I drink chocolate milk?"

"They are noticing and commenting and learning about the categories we describe as race," said Beverly, "though they don't understand those categories in the way that adults do. So, if we wait until they're teenagers, they will already have ideas well formed. You have more sophisticated conversations with 10-year-olds than you do with 4-year-olds, and you have more sophisticated conversations with 17-year-olds than you do with 7-year-olds, but if you wait till they're 14 or 17, you've lost a lot of time. We need to start the conversations with preschool."

Henry has no shortage of questions, and I'm okay with that. I'm remembering now how much I loved this type of conversation with my sisters' kids and grandkids. I've always loved the way children ask questions that bring truth out of confusion like an orchid from the swamp.

"Where's your dad?"

"He's in Heaven." And he's in me. And he's in every Black person who ever rode the bus in Baton Rouge.

"Why is the sky blue?"

"Because of the way light waves travel through the atmosphere." And because we see it that way. Because someone taught us to call that color *blue*.

"Why did dinosaurs die?"

"An asteroid hit Earth, and the environment changed. Plants and animals that found nourishment lived, and anything that didn't find nourishment died." And so it is with ideologies, demagogues, and dreams.

"Will you go on the trampoline with me?"

"No." Because the lessons we learn through pain— these are the lessons that pierce our illusions and stay with us.

The calamitous way in which 2020 unfurled—the cascading consequences of fear, greed, and shortsightedness—forced open the eyes of a generation born to a dying planet. Our young people now know that they live in a fluctuating zone of social unrest, ecological trauma, personal anxiety, and communal illness that will continue to shift and liquefy beneath our feet until we come together in a unified effort to stabilize it.

There's no doubt in my mind; we are nurturing another Obama, cultivating the next Mandela, growing a new Boudica. Those children are out there somewhere right now, on the street marching, doing kindergarten on Zoom, playing Fortnite, or learning to trick-or-treat in a world where everyone is already wearing a mask. But we can't afford to wait for them to find their way to the future. The crucial task before us now is to protect the world into which they'll emerge so that when their moment comes, they still have a democracy, a climate, and a humanity worth fighting for.

It's time we outgrow our need for a celebrity messiah. We must step up and become the savior the world is waiting for. It's our turn to envision sweeping change and our responsibility to engage in sustainable, nonviolent disruption until we make that change happen. We must commit ourselves to revolutionary acts of covenant and absolution and end this uncivil war, which is truly the most idiotic conflict in the history of mankind. It would be laughable at times, if it wasn't so damn heartbreaking.

In her novel *Their Eyes Were Watching God*, Zora Neale Hurston wrote: "There are years that ask questions and years that answer." With the arrival of that first slave ship on the Virginia shore, the Year of Our Lord 1619 begged a simple question we have yet to answer:

How does this end?

Choosing to build an economy on the backs of abducted slaves and indentured immigrants, our forebears embedded dangerous fault lines deep beneath the crust of a towering nation that would evolve out of tyranny, through struggle, into greatness. They knowingly begot an ethos of denial and imparity, never imagining or needing to imagine the cost to their own descendants or the progeny of the people they exploited. They may have hoped, but no way did they predict that the United States would eventually stand as the world's last remaining superpower, the teeming fundament of a vast global economy.

All their asking years focused on a ravenous acquisition of goods and a grasping thirst for power: *How far? How much? How much more? What's in it for me?* We can undo exactly none of the havoc they wreaked. We can only move forward with our own interrogative life, asking, *Why not? What if? For whom?*

We the People of These United States, entrenched as we are in our uncivil war, are not the living light of democracy we've traditionally fancied ourselves to be. Our lives have become an ad space where fear, greed, and fascism are marketed. The rest of the world is averting their eyes with shock and dismay. I say this not because I hate my country but because I love my country, because I am willing to fight for my country and speak hard truth on my country's behalf. I say this because we genuinely need to know: How—*how*—does this end?

We know how it *doesn't* end. It doesn't end with the savage putting down of a slave uprising in Louisiana or the tear gassing of protesters on the streets of Washington, DC. It doesn't end with half measures, murders, marches, political correction, token wokeness, or a ceding of the soul that engenders neighbor-hate and self-loathing. All these have been tried. Instead of answers, every wasted arrow that sought to silence rather than solve this problem hammered the question home, over and over, an endless drumbeat:

How does this end?

How does this end?

How does this end?

People, there *is* no end. The answer is a new beginning, and that can be forged only in the crucible of compassionately radical *change*.

Imagine what could happen if we reverse-engineer the society we want to live in and speak that into being. Imagine what could be accomplished if we call up the powers of technology and industry—the wealth of resources that came out of our twisted beginning—and judiciously apply all that to equitable good. Imagine the bridges we could build when we ourselves become the conduit between what was and what can be.

Before the 2008 election, Oprah Winfrey told Barack Obama that she'd heard him speak and said, "I think this is the one."

"I think I'm one of the ones," said Obama.

He saw the long game, the vast arc of history in which even the greatest among us can play only a small part. Like Obama, I grew up in the slipstream of progressive thought initiated by John Lewis, MLK, and Harvey Milk. We've been around this block before. We've seen America's capacity for progress, but we've learned that any progress made by Black people in the United States is followed by a backlash of wounded fury from those unable to imagine a future beyond our current caste system of White supremacy.

In the final pages of *The Fire Next Time,* James Baldwin holds out hope for the "relatively conscious whites and the relatively conscious blacks, who must, like lovers, insist on, or create, the consciousness of the others." But in that hope, there's a guarded undercurrent of skepticism, the ever-present *SET.* I think he knew there would be a next time, and a next-next time, and a time after that, because the next times will never end until Black people reject their numb complacency and White people reject their entitled privilege.

For a long time now, we've been in need of the sort of intervention that places an addict on the road to recovery. There is potential for that rock-bottom moment in the pandemic of 2020, and it might be a long time before such a moment comes around again. Will we take the first step—admit we have a problem—and begin the hard work of our national salvation, or will we return to the comfort of the status quo like a junkie to the needle?

We are capable of releasing the burden of racism. We are capable of dialogue that fosters intersectional alliances. We are capable of educating future generations with self-honesty and shared humanity. We are capable of intelligent, organized activism that pushes toward a common goal. We can be simultaneously fearless about our future and truthful about our past. We can be equally conscious of our country's failings and proud of our country's progress. The very essence of progress is to build a bridge that takes us from here to there, but what good is progress without healing?

I keep thinking about John Lewis on Bloody Sunday in the context of recent efforts to have the Edmund Pettus Bridge renamed for him. Progress is John Lewis standing on the Edmund Pettus Bridge. Healing is you and me standing on the John Lewis Bridge. We can get there—we *can*—if we're willing to do the work. History is always *now* for somebody. Why not us? If every one of us is willing to be "one of the ones," we have it in us to meet this moment together, feel its mighty sway, and emerge from the chaos to craft a more just and loving world.

The Old Testament prophet Malachi spoke of a refining fire, a furnace of affliction that purifies the soul like silver and gold. Such is the flame that burns within us now, reducing convention and injustice to ash, lighting our way forward to a new way of being.

We are the inferno in which Baldwin placed his faith. *This* is the fire.

Let the last next time be now.

Appendix

READ

Notes of a Native Son by James Baldwin (Beacon Press, 1955)

The Fire Next Time by James Baldwin (Dial Press, 1963)

If Beale Street Could Talk by James Baldwin (Dial Press, 1974)

Black Girls Learn Love Hard by Ras Baraka (Moore Black Press, 2006)

My Song: A Memoir of Art, Race, and Defiance by Harry Belafonte and Michael Shnayerson (Knopf, 2011)

Toms, Coons, Mulattoes, Mammies, and Bucks: An Interpretive History of Blacks in American Films by Donald Bogle (Bloomsbury Academic, 1973)

The Essays of Warren Buffett: Lessons for Corporate America by Warren Buffett, ed. Lawrence A. Cunningham (Wright Publishing, 2008)

Open Season: Legalized Genocide of Colored People by Ben Crump (HarperCollins, 2021)

Lena by Lena Horne and Richard Schickel (Doubleday, 1965)

Their Eyes Were Watching God by Zora Neale Hurston (Lippincott, 1937)

A Sin by Any Other Name: Reckoning with Racism and the Heritage of the South by Robert W. Lee IV (Penguin Random House, 2019)

Long Walk to Freedom: The Autobiography of Nelson Mandela by Nelson Mandela (Little, Brown, 1994)

American Uprising: The Untold Story of America's Largest Slave Revolt by Daniel Rasmussen (HarperCollins, 2011)

The People Are Going to Rise Like the Waters upon Your Shore: A Story of American Rage by Jared Yates Sexton (Counterpoint Press, 2017)

American Rule: How a Nation Conquered the World but Failed Its People by Jared Yates Sexton (Dutton/ Penguin Random House, 2020)

Rise Up: Confronting a Country at the Crossroads by Al Sharpton (HarperCollins, 2020)

Migrating to the Movies: Cinema and Black Urban Modernity by Jaqueline Najuma Stewart (University of California Press, 2005)

Why Are All the Black Kids Sitting Together in the

Cafeteria? And Other Conversations About Race by Beverly Daniel Tatum (Basic Books, 1997)

The Warmth of Other Suns: The Epic Story of America's Great Migration by Isabel Wilkerson (Random House, 2010)

Caste: The Origins of Our Discontents by Isabel Wilkerson (Penguin Random House, 2020)

Fear: Trump in the White House by Bob Woodward (Simon & Schuster, 2018)

Rage by Bob Woodward (Simon & Schuster, 2020)

All the President's Men by Bob Woodward and Carl Bernstein (Simon & Schuster, 1974)

LISTEN

Podcasts

Silence Is Not an Option, hosted by Don Lemon (CNN Audio). 2020 episodes:

"Why Not Being Racist Is Not Enough," with Professor Ibram X. Kendi and Professor Christopher Petrella (June 18, 2020)

"Beyond Mammy: Misrepresentation in Film," with Don's mother, Katherine Clark, and TCM's Jacqueline Stewart (June 25, 2020)

"Schooling the System," with Professor Sheneka Williams (July 2, 2020)

"Monumental Conversations," with descendants of a Confederate general and Jared Yates Sexton (July 9, 2020)

"Defining What Matters," with recent college graduate Kennedy Mitchum and linguist John McWhorter (July 16, 2020)

"Finding Common Ground," with Kareem Abdul-Jabbar, historian Marc Dollinger, and political strategist Ginna Green (July 23, 2020)

"Reimagining the Police," with Newark Mayor Ras Baraka, Eric Garner's mother, Gwen Carr, and Professor Chenjerai Kumanyika (July 30, 2020)

"American Caste with Isabel Wilkerson," on the Pulitzer Prize–winning author's new book, *Caste: The Origins of Our Discontents* (August 6, 2020)

"Do Black Lives Matter in Sports?," with sports journalist William C. Rhoden (August 13, 2020)

"Clearing the Air: Environmental Justice," with environmental justice advocate Mustafa Santiago Ali (August 20, 2020)

"The Color of Love," with CNN's *United Shades of America* W. Kamau Bell and Don's fiancé, Tim Malone (August 27, 2020)

"Raising an Antiracist Generation," with clinical psychologist and race relations expert Beverly Daniel Tatum (September 10, 2020)

"Can You Vote Your Way to Change?," with activist Daud Mumin and Black Lives Matter co-founder LaTosha Brown (October 15, 2020)

"Yes, Voter Suppression Is Alive and Well," with voter protection specialist Josh Levin and Professor Carol Anderson (October 22, 2020)

"Blaxit," with historian Kevin Gaines and author Tiffanie Drayton (October 29, 2020)

"Black Women Did That," with Black Lives Matter co-founder LaTosha Brown and Congresswoman Frederica Wilson (November 12, 2020)

Other Audio

YouTube, *Uncomfortable Conversations with a Black Man,* hosted by Emmanuel Acho

Spotify Studio, *Jemele Hill Is Unbothered,* hosted by Jemele Hill

Gimlet Media, *Uncivil,* hosted by Chenjerai Kumanyika

National Action Network, *Keepin' It Real with Reverend Al Sharpton*

WATCH

Dave Chappelle, *The Age of Spin: Dave Chappelle Live at the Hollywood Palladium,* distributed by Netflix, 2017

CNN's *Cuomo Prime Time,* hosted by Chris Cuomo, also
a podcast on CNN Audio
Jordan Klepper, *The Opposition with Jordan Klepper,*
Comedy Central, 2017–2018
Al Sharpton, *Politics Nation,* MSNBC, first aired in 2011

ENGAGE

All Voting Is Local, AllVotingIsLocal.org
Black Lives Matter, BlackLivesMatter.com
From Privilege to Progress, FromPrivilegeToProgress.org

Acknowledgments

The work I'm called to and the life I love are made possible by a circle of wonderful people.

My mom, Katherine Clark, is my one-woman focus group, my rock, and my North Star. She carried me inside her and carries me to this day. Mom and my sister, Yma — that's my girls. No one could ask for a truer sounding board. To my family — Trushaad, Cairo, Ashleigh, Kimberly, Katherine, and Morris — I love you all. Love and thanks also to the Malone family for bringing me into the fold. Thank you all for keeping me grounded.

It's a privilege to work with my colleagues at CNN: Jeff Zucker, one of the most courageous people in broadcasting, inspires me to do my best work and gives me the editorial freedom to do it. Executive producers Maria Spinella and Philippa Holland move mountains with unfailing grace and astonishing speed. Chris Cuomo is my partner in crime, my favorite person to agree and disagree with. Shanique Clarke keeps all the trains running. Writer Susan Lay gets me like she has a direct uplink to my brain. Maybe she'll help me find words to tell you all how much I appreciate you.

Sincere thanks to all the dedicated professionals who helped me get this book right and get it into the hands of readers: my agent Jay Sures at UTA for helping me steer my energy toward the greatest good I can do in the world; Ryan Hayden for planting the seed; Byrd Leavell and Albert Lee for finding the best possible publishing home for me. Thanks to the entire team at Little, Brown and Company: my editor, Bruce Nichols, for his vision, insight, and faith in me as the messenger for this moment; deputy publisher Craig Young; publicity director Sabrina Callahan; and their amazing staff, including assistant editor Miya Kumangai and senior production editor Pat Jalbert-Levine. Thanks to Joni Rodgers at Westport Lighthouse Writers Retreat for creative development. I've enjoyed our late-night bonding sessions. Thanks also to Joni's agent, Cindi Davis-Andress, and to Patty Lewis Lott for research.

I'm humbly grateful to all the artists, experts, activists, and other extraordinary people who've shared their stories with me on my show and podcast, and to all the viewers and listeners who open their minds, keep me honest, and continually challenge me to listen harder, think deeper, and reach farther.

Acknowledgments

Tim Malone (soon to be Tim Malone Lemon), I kept you for last, because you are the sanctuary I need at the end of every day. You keep me young, renew my faith in unconditional love, and uphold my belief in two fundamental truths: love is love and family is everything. I'll tell you the rest when I get home.

Don Lemon
New York City
Spring 2021

Index

Index

Index

Index

About the Author

Don Lemon anchors CNN *Tonight with Don Lemon* and led the network's coverage of the police-involved death of George Floyd and the protests and riots that followed. A news veteran of Chicago, he joined CNN in September 2006 and has reported and anchored on-the-scene for many breaking news stories, including the Charleston, South Carolina, church shooting; the death of Freddie Gray while in police custody; the shooting of unarmed teenager Michael Brown in Ferguson, Missouri; and the George Zimmerman trial; among many others. Lemon is known for holding politicians and public officials accountable and for his compassionate, intuitive interviews with everyday people.